40 Years and Counting

Teesdale & Weardale
Search & Mountain Rescue Team
www.TWSMRT.org.uk

Compiled by Kathrine High

Foreword by Matt Baker

Edited by Chris Roberts and Anthony Tubbs

Dedication

To all those Team members past and present who have given, and continue to give their time and commitment to the Teesdale & Weardale Search & Mountain Rescue Team.

In Memory

GE Hulatt - 09.08.87 - Founder Member
F Stubbs - 28.12.88 - Founder Member
M Burgess - 01.08.89
T Buffey - 30.09.89 - Founder Member
D Robinson - 29.08.92 - Founder Member
E Richardson - 30.01.94 - Founder Member
A Box - 17.08.94
D Snell - 15.10.97
S White - 10.02.02
D Coggins - 03.09.03 - Founder Member
Bert Patchett - 10.03.07 - Vice President
Ken Saxby - 27.06.09 - Vice President

ISBN 978-0-9564726-0-1

Published in 2010 by Teesdale?& Weardale Search & Mountain Rescue Team

Designed and Produced by CJBS Design

Email: chris.bartles-smith@hotmail.com   **Tel:** 07969 993626

Contents

Foreword

Written by Matt Baker

Wrapped in a waterproof bivvy bag on the hillside of a wooded valley, anyone could be forgiven for wondering why, for the second time, they've been voluntarily abandoned and left in total isolation waiting for the imminent arrival of the Search and Rescue Team. But, I'm part of a vital training exercise, and soon I hope my crossword or soggy novel will be sharply interrupted by the presence of a pair of furry ears popping up over the gorse.

My connection with search and rescue started back in 2004 whilst working on Blue Peter, when my Border Collie Meg was in pup. She's from a strong line of working sheep dogs and I wanted her offspring to follow in their ancestors paw prints and lead active and useful lives. Search and rescue was at the top of my list.

Meg's pups left our farm in Durham one by one after being tested and selected by their prospective recipients and of course I was delighted when one gentle black and white pup was chosen as a new recruit for SARDA Southern Scotland. She joined the ranks at 10 weeks old and, as with her brothers and sisters, our Blue Peter cameras followed her progress as 'Corrie' as she was named (a Scottish valley) and her handler James Cole took various search and rescue tests to qualify into what is now one of the most successful man and dog teams working nationwide today.

I have been fortunate enough with my job to travel extensively, far and wide away from the dales where I grew up right around the world from Australia to Outer Mongolia. Yet I still struggle to find a landscape that can rival that of my beloved County Durham. From the River Tees and the River Wear, which have carved out valleys, rich in geology, ravines, gorges and waterfalls, unforgiving high fells in the West that rise through 'England's last wilderness' with plateaus, approaching 3,000 feet above the coastal communities of the North Sea.

For some it's an adventure playground and for others it's just home, but it's a challenging environment with more than enough opportunity for folk to find themselves in trouble. Our rugged and varied landscape is given yet more character by the unpredictable northern weather, which as a boy was measured by how many top coats we put on. It goes without saying what an incredible service the Mountain Rescue Team provide and have done for decades. For 40 years my local group, the Teesdale and Weardale Search and Mountain Rescue Team, have been selflessly pushing themselves to the limits, co-ordinating, searching and providing vital care for those in need at the drop of a hat.

So, back to the training exercise on a 3 top coat day. My thoughts are interrupted with a burst of energy as Dan, the Rescue Dog bounds up and turns on a sixpence to return barking to his handler. I'm found, I'm safe and no longer alone in the elements.

I never tire of witnessing this heroism, as this team of volunteers is ready and willing to take to the wilderness 24hrs a day in all weathers so that we can continue to explore the beauty of real Britain.

Teesdale & Weardale Search and Mountain Rescue Team

by the Chief Constable, Durham Constabulary

I am delighted to be afforded the opportunity to congratulate the Teesdale and Weardale Search and Mountain Rescue Team on achieving forty years of continuous volunteer service to the community.

As some will be aware, the Team were established in 1968 following a tragedy earlier that year. Two young men from Shildon lost their lives when they were swept away by the River Tees, whilst negotiating Maize Beck in Upper Teesdale.

Following that tragedy, members of the local community recognised a need to form a specialist search team and it is as a result of their vision that the rescue team were formed from committed and enthusiastic volunteers.

I am proud that in 1968 Durham Constabulary established links with the Team which have been maintained throughout and that those strong links skill exist today.

In fact, Durham Constabulary has called upon the Team on many occasions over those forty years to assist in rescue or search operations, often in very difficult and demanding conditions. I am left in no doubt that their contribution, dedication and professionalism in such operations has saved many lives.

Significantly all team members are volunteers who frequently put their own lives on hold, whilst responding to calls for assistance with extraordinary commitment and dedication.

No doubt many would wish to express their individual thanks to the Team for their efforts over the years, but may I, on behalf of Durham Constabulary personnel, offer my sincere appreciation for their dedication and commitment over the past forty years and wish the Team every success for the future.

Jon Stoddart Q.P.M., B.A. (Hons)
Chief Constable

Team on Excercise in Tan Hill area

Introduction

'Without the team…there is no team!'

Wise words (!!) from Russ Warne

The Teesdale and Weardale Search and Mountain Rescue Team celebrated 40 years of service in 2008 and amongst other celebrations that took place they also decided to mark the occasion with a book. Not only is this to commemorate the anniversary but also to raise some much needed funds. This book was a fantastic idea that hopes to give you, the reader, an insight into the workings of the team.

Established in 1968, sustained success is largely due to the efforts and commitment of highly skilled team members, both past and present. Currently a 50-strong team of both male and female volunteers, all with ordinary full time jobs - just an everyday bunch of people you would pass in the supermarket. However, they are special because this bunch of people from differing backgrounds, willingly give their time to be on call 24 hours a day, 7 days a week, all year round. They could get a callout in the middle of the night or at the most inconvenient time, in awful weather, but they grab their kit and they're off. At times searches can last for long periods, with some even spanning over a number of days, in some the most remote countryside in England. At other times, the team could be stood down before members even arrive at the RV point, so they simply turn the car around and go back home.

The title 'Mountain Rescue' suggests exactly that, however it isn't always about searching and rescuing intrepid explorers of the North Pennines. There are other reasons this lot has to leave the comfort of their beds or disrupt their working day and family events. The Team, in many cases, supports the police in urban searches. You may have seen them traipsing through Durham City centre mid-afternoon in search of a lost child or a vulnerable person suffering from Alzheimer's disease or someone else. It can be an odd sight, seeing members of the Team fully kitted out in walking boots and a backpack and radio, seemingly mingling amongst the bustle of a busy street as if they have just been teleported from the Base Camp at Everest!

One Team member from Sunderland often hears the remark, 'But there are no mountains in Sunderland'. No - there are not. Nor are there in Durham City, Darlington, Peterlee or Easington for that matter. However these areas have surprisingly difficult and wild terrain – for example searching the River Wear in Durham or the Denes in the East of the County. The area of the North Pennines covered by the Team, is an area of high Fells and is very remote with challenging terrain. The point however, is that the Team are diverse in their role as a search and rescue organisation. The Team has developed and established the operations over the last 40 years through hard work, dedication and professionalism. Over this period, the Team has established strong links with the police, who have overall responsibility for missing persons and instigate the Team callout.

Although the Team is part of the emergency services, and works closely in partnership with other such organisations, it is entirely independent and voluntary. As a registered charity, it depends on sponsorship and the generosity of the public for donations, as it receives no central government funding or subsidies. It is responsible for holding fundraising events, this book being one of them. Financial support is essential as it pays for the running of its' emergency vehicles, provision and upkeep of lifesaving equipment, on-going training and supporting the Youth Team.

A need for the Team was established over 40 years ago and that need continues today and to the future. Without continued financial support, coming in from the kind donations and generosity of the public, then the Team would cease to exist. So next time you see the Team Members fundraising or holding a tin at a Street collection in your area, just remember one thing, for whatever personal reason each member joined the team, they have these things in common - they all do it for free and they all do it to save lives!

A Team briefing in the early years

Rescue excercise at High Force, River Tees

Team on Excercise in Upper Weardale

History of the Team

They were wet, cold and hopelessly lost. In the fading light and driving rain, one man could just make out the fearful, pained expression in his brother-in -law's face. In total blackness, gale force winds and near arctic temperatures they tried to take bearings but gentle becks had become loud raging torrents. They seemed to be trapped. At 10pm a weak signal appeared on the mobile phone, a chance to get help, a call to home, just a bit of information, but the signal was lost. At the rescue centre in Barnard Castle, Team Leaders and the Police worked urgently to try to piece together the position of the men. Soon after midnight 20 volunteers and their search dog Meg were beginning to search, moving westwards on both sides of the Tees and the Pennine Way from Cronkley. Seven hours later, Team members were wading through treacherous waters in Swarfbeck, trying to keep in sight of Megs' black and white markings – she had found the missing men and was leading the Team in. Everyone huddled together in a large survival tent, the missing men treated for hyperthermia and a Sea King helicopter summoned from RAF Boulmer.

The searchers that night had passed the spot where, in March 1968, two young men tragically lost their lives in terrible circumstances. One slipped and drowned trying to cross Maize Beck, the other, left by friends, consequently went missing, and his body found the next morning. Both men were members of the same party of youths out on a fell-walking expedition near High Cup Nick in Teesdale. The weather hadn't favoured the trip and the group soon found themselves amid fog, rain, strong winds and even patches of snow. It was stormy and many locals at the time agreed the treacherous conditions were exceptional; the River Tees had risen higher than anyone had ever witnessed and the speed with which it flowed was incredible. The other participants of the outing were alive but suffering from exposure, they were cold, stiff, experiencing cramping and understandably frightened. Fog prevented them from finding their way back and they knew the nearest house was three and half-hours away. The walkers were in an extreme situation and because there was no local organised group available to help more quickly, a specialist force from outside Durham was called, in order to find them. However, this didn't stop the determined efforts of the founding members of the Team and this event led to the formation of the Upper Teesdale and Weardale Fell Rescue Team.

Nationwide, at this time, a number of Mountain Rescue teams were in operation, including in the neighbouring areas of the Lake District and Northumberland, but the occurrences of that unfortunate weekend only highlighted the necessity for a team in and around County Durham, particularly in Upper Teesdale and the North Pennines. So, just three months later, on 19th June 1968, one of the members, Tom Buffey, held a public meeting in the High Force Hotel with a view to discuss the possibility of forming a local fell rescue team. A subsequent inaugural meeting in September held at the same venue proved just as successful and in attendance were around 60 people. Present were members of the Northumberland Mountain Rescue Team, including its chairman, as were representatives of local authorities and rambling organisations. A working committee was put in place with Tom appointed as chairman, and his aim was to ensure the whole community was involved in its rescue efforts. It was also made clear that anyone capable of assisting the organisation could help, and it was deemed inappropriate to apply an upper age limit to Team members as this might deter those interested from volunteering. These sentiments remain very much with the organisation today.

Although the meeting at the hotel was the official birth of the Team, the idea had come about during a previous chance encounter between Tom and another founding member, John L Bumby. The pair found themselves envisaging a rescue team over a hot drink just weeks after the tragedy of Maize Beck. Here is a personal recollection by John Bumby himself.

'The team concept was conceived in early April 1968 on the front seat of a steamed up Land Rover. I was enjoying a solitary uneventful day wandering around a well-loved area of Upper Teesdale, beyond Birkdale Farm. I had left home at Stanhope Castle School in warm spring sunshine but by early afternoon snow flurries coming over Meldon Hill took on a more threatening nature. A recent tragedy and rescue incident on the Maize Beck a few weeks previously came to mind, and I decided to retrace my steps to Langdon Beck. Instead of following the banks of the River Tees, I clambered up the side on Cauldron Snout and made for Cow Green Lane. The Widdy Bank track was well covered with snow by this time and I was becoming increasingly wet and uncomfortable. Having been without shelter or human contact all day, I came across a lone-parked Land Rover at grid reference 817308. As I approached, I managed to read through the swirling snow an intriguing logo on its side – "Cow Green Reservoir Site Research Officer". The occupant, Tom Buffey, made me welcome. During our chat and shared coffee, I noticed he had a Mountain Rescue badge on his jacket. He told me he had been a member of a rescue Team in Northumberland, but had given up his business on Tyneside to take up the research post at the Cow Green site, an appointment for which he was obviously well qualified. Having learned of his rescue experiences, our conversation turned to the fact there was no rescue team in our area. This was underlined by the tragic accident in Maize Beck. I remember this incident was controlled by RAF Leeming Mountain Rescue Team (MRT) assisted by several Teams from the surrounding districts. There was an obvious lack of cover from our own area. Tom and I agreed that a local team was not only essential but also already feasible. Some names were mentioned: Denis Coggins already had rescue equipment at High Force Hotel; Don Robinson, assistant warden at Langdon Beck Youth Hostel, had vast local knowledge of places and people. Another shared acquaintance in Upper Teesdale was Dr Margaret Bradshaw who had carried out research in the remote parts of the fells over the years. I was aware that an obvious candidate for Team membership would be Ray Dent from Glenwhilt Farm in Weardale who was already the supervisor of the Mountain Rescue Council (MRC) sub-post at his location. Through his experience with the Northumberland Team, Tom had developed close relationships with Tom McGeorge, the then Chairman of North East Search and Rescue Association (NESRA), and Fred Stubbs, its secretary. Similarly, he knew Ken Saxby of Search and Rescue Dog Association (SARDA) as well as senior Police Officers in Bishop Auckland and Richmond. Thus, our chance meeting ended – creative ideas shared and discussed, and a way forward agreed. I left Tom sitting in his cosy cab, and as I made my way down Peg Horn Lane I wondered if this could be the start of 'something big'.

A steering committee was then formed and we held a series of meetings at Tom's home and at High Force Hotel to draw up our constitution and establish our own boundaries. After our intentions had been ratified by the MRC (Mountain Rescue Council) by mid September 1968, the Association was formed. The area to be covered by the "Upper Teesdale and Weardale Fell Rescue Association" was large: the catchment area of the River Tees west of Barnard Castle and the catchment area of the River Wear west of Wolsingham. We also included the southern part of the catchment area of the River Derwent west of Muggleswick. The Association would have two sections – one for each dale. They would be able to operate independently or together. Each section would have a leader – Tom Buffey for Teesdale and Ray Dent for Weardale. Each leader would have a small team of trained specialists who could deal with any emergency rapidly, organise, and lead larger search parties, should a wide search be required. Larger search parties were to be made up of local farmers, shepherds, gamekeepers and local residents. This is the reason we became an 'association' of local people who collectively had immense knowledge of the area within our boundaries. We would also assist, of course, neighbouring Teams if requested.

I have three special reasons to be proud of my association with TWSMRT – the three members I enlisted. Mike Stansfield was invited to bring his climbing skills to the Team on joining the staff at Stanhope Castle. He was outstanding on one particular occasion when almost single-handedly, he carried out the rescue of a visitor to High Force who had fallen over the top of the falls and had managed to scramble onto a ledge on the south side. Secondly, I remember my good friend and colleague, Stan White, who was woodwork instructor at Stanhope Castle. He was no fells man at that time but was still approached to become a Team member. He agreed and we benefited from his enthusiasm, his willingness to try anything, and his many talents. He had a brilliant command of the English language, but I fear that some of his vocabulary had developed in his workshop, probably whilst using a large hammer and tiny nails. Stan became a legend in his role as Team Secretary. At the very formation of the Association, I suggested to my faithful friend, Chris Scott, that he too should join the Association. This great guy has served throughout with unlimited loyalty. He became Team Treasurer – holder of the purse strings and amazingly adept at tying knots. Sadly, recent ill health has prevented him from tramping his beloved fells, but after forty years, he continues to give much of his time and energy for the benefit of the Team in his quiet, modest and most efficient manner. Thanks to the dedicated efforts of so many fine people, that chance meeting forty years ago at GR 817308 did prove to be the start of something big'.

By mid-October, fifty people had already volunteered their services, training had begun, and after a successful first year, the Team had more than doubled bringing the total amount of active members to an impressive 117.

The original purpose of the rescue Team was to ensure that people who were injured, lost in darkness, or freezing conditions on the fells, would have a reliable local force that could save them from the exposure of the elements. The fell rescue did exactly what it said on the tin; recover casualties from the hills around the Wear and Tees with great team spirit, limited communications and poor equipment. For the most part of the 70s, callouts were rare, and much of the time was spent training and fundraising, but in 1979 heavy snowfall created havoc on the dales roads. Drifts of over six feet high caused one male driver to abandon his vehicle and set home on foot. His family raised the alarm when he failed to return home and this was the Teams' first callout that took them away from the open hillside. Although not a major incident like the ones that followed, it still demonstrated the capabilities of the Team. This wasn't to be recognised fully, however, until much later and more so when the methods in which they used for search and rescue developed.

Developments

The early callouts for the Team were largely recoveries of casualties from (allegedly) known locations. They were rescues on, and evacuations from, the fell. However, because perhaps the person going to call for help did not know their exact position, or a whole party were overdue and 'lost', sometimes searches were needed. Most often, either by the description of route or lie of the land, or even the type of grasses near where the injured person was left, someone with local knowledge could pinpoint quite well where the casualty would be. Sometimes a walker was long overdue and when an immediate search of footpaths, or shelter points had not turned up the casualty, the Team would have to resort to searching. The method adopted by the Team in a search was suggested to them by the police and refined by Dave Thompson (Team Controller) and his deputy Ken Saxby. This was the technique of 'line searching', which had evolved in Police forces largely to search for evidence but equally applied to 'manhunts'. The previous search technique of the line search was proving to be too time consuming out on the fell, difficult to control in all but the best weather conditions, and very de-motivating. The searcher would often spend more time and attention trying to stay in position in the line as the ground underfoot twisted and turned rather than actually searching for the missing person. Systems of signals, whistles, CB radios and group leaders charging up and down the line still often couldn't stop one or more searchers from the end of the line heading off down into a valley, or sometimes over a ridge and down into the next valley!

A change to this standard method began during the early part of the 1980s. The work of Rick Lavalla and other professional search and rescuers from the National Parks in the United States was introduced to the UK. Following major incidents like the eruption of Mount St Helen in Washington State, a number of individuals were employed to sort out a method for search and rescue. We began to adopt some of their ideas to our own situation and particularly in NESRA and East Cumbria Search Panel (ECP) training. One of their key ideas we adopted was the effectiveness of using small search groups. These groups are sent to locations and terrain where there is a higher probability that a missing person could have had a mishap, or might have gone to ground. They also search fence lines or streams which can be used as a natural boundary or guide for someone to follow when 'lost'.

Increasingly the Team found themselves being called to look for those, other than fell walkers, who had become lost on the fringes of the fells; injured on the steep ground along the Tees or Wear; or in abandoned quarries or mineshafts. The police recognised more and more that there was a group of keen, fit, well-organised and skilled individuals, all of whom had basic first aid training. They were effectively managed with systems that allowed them to be deployed in small search groups rapidly into areas of difficult or hazardous terrain. They also proved successful in locating a casualty, stabilising any injury, then extricating and evacuating from the most difficult circumstances in all weathers, day or night. Working relationships with senior officers developed and the Team began to be called to try to find missing, often vulnerable people on the urban fringes. The Team was evolving from 'Fell Rescue' to 'Search and Rescue'.

There were a number of major events in the late 1980s and early 1990s that catalysed this change. The first was Lockerbie.

Lockerbie Air Disaster 21st December 1988

I was down in Somerset celebrating Christmas with my family when I saw on the news the events unfolding in Lockerbie. There had been an explosion on Pan Am 103 with 258 passengers and 12 crew on board 31,000 feet above Lockerbie just after 7 pm on the evening of 21st December 1988. The following day when the scale of the tragedy gradually became clear, I telephoned Team Secretary Stan White to find out if there had been any MR involvement. He advised me that SARDA had been called to the area around Lockerbie to assist. Stan phoned back on Christmas Eve to say that in addition to SARDA, Northumbria police had now instigated a NESRA call out.

A farmer from the west side of Kielder Water had called police when he had gone down his drive to find large amounts of 'litter' blown into hedges and trees. He initially thought that vandals had overturned his bins, only later realising that it was lightweight aircraft debris. We were to meet very early on the morning of the 27th on the Green in West Auckland to go in convoy to the village of Bellingham in Northumberland for a 7am briefing. In all 37 members of the Team met on the Green that day and we realised how important involvement in such a major event could be for the Team. Like everyone else, I had no idea what we were to face in the coming days and weeks but unlike the rest of the Team I had a 320-mile drive first.

In the first hour of the search, the enormity of the task began to emerge. At the briefing we were given a large sector of the west end of Kielder Forest to try to find any 'bits' from the aircraft, we had walked into our first forest clearing where, like blown snow in a winter storm forming drifts in the lee of the wind, honeycomb plastic pieces were on the ground and in the trees. Within minutes, the black bin bag I had taken with me was full. I walked back out to the Control vehicle to talk to Dave Thompson, to try to give him a sense of what we might be facing and the need to get a large supply of bin bags! We also discussed the importance of marking up the bags with the location of the finds and who collected the evidence. We could only systematically try to cover the tracks, firebreaks and clearings. The nature of the debris on the ground changed as we moved south, as well as the honeycomb plastic we began to find odd fragments of clothing, shreds of documents or papers and larger pieces of plastic or shards of aluminium. Fortunately for us, they were all pieces of an inanimate aircraft. I felt relieved that we were not facing anything like the nightmare horror that surrounded the village of Lockerbie. We were not to be immune from the human tragedy however.

It may have been the second day when my group and that of Ian Findlay's found ourselves at either end of a very large clearing. One member of my group called me to come over, as I walked towards him he was looking up into a tree transfixed and motionless, silent. There hanging a few feet above him in the Pine tree was a tiny, one-piece 'baby grow' infant suit. Other torn bits of infant wear lay around but it was the way that the undamaged baby grow hung lifelessly in the tree that connected us for the first time with those on the plane. Worse still, a few minutes later nearby, was a children's storybook lying open on the ground. I don't think I was alone in choking back tears.

As the days went by I became more involved with the NESRA search management group coordinating the search and, although on the fringe, I gained some very valuable experience in the organisation of a large scale search. It was becoming clear that there were two swathes of debris that had been blown by westerly winds across Northumberland. We were mapping where debris had been found. The two distinct swathes running from west to east were gradually fanning out towards the coast. We were able to project where debris would be found and to draw out search areas where there was a greater likelihood of finding evidence. Back on the ground, we began to find personal effects like passports, wallets, credit cards, and letters and in one location a package that could have changed our lives. We were searching an area of fairly open heath and scrub. Dave Forster called me over to look at a package about the size of a shoebox. It was something wrapped up in heavy-duty brown paper, tied very securely and addressed to a bank in New York. Just one corner of the package was slightly torn. I tried to see what was inside, curious; somehow, the rip in the package got just that little bit wider. In that corner alone was a very large wad of dollar bills packed very tightly together. Dave and I have often tried to guess at how much in total the package contained, and what we could have spent the money on but like every other piece of debris evidence, large or small, it was bagged, labelled and handed in at the end of the day in the school hall in Bellingham.

As Stuart Leishman, the Team Press Officer said, at the end of the two-week search, 'We've had some good times and some dreadful times but the best thing of all is that the fell rescue system really works. They called us in to do a job and day after day, we've proved that we can do it. It makes all the training worthwhile'. Lockerbie allowed the Teams of the North East to demonstrate to the police that we were very effective search organisations.

Changing from the Fell Rescue Association to the Search and Rescue Team

At the end of 1980s, the Team was beginning to consider that the name 'Fell Rescue' no longer reflected the true nature of the wide variety of work that we were undertaking. An event that tested the depth of resolve of the Team in this period and showed the public how effective the Team could be in the most extreme conditions took place over a weekend in early December 1990. This event also made the Team reassess the way in which it dealt with the media.

In the 1980s, we were often described as a group of willing volunteers who came out of nowhere to deal with a fell rescue then to merge back into the ether. We had an annual sponsored walk to raise funds and sometimes a press article generated by the occasional donation from a local group. As the police are in charge of the search callouts, they also historically handled the media. This meant that Team rarely gained direct recognition for their involvement , other than through a reference to 'volunteers' assisting with a rescue, which generally meant that the Team's initial involvement in some search and rescue operations was not highlighted.

The blizzard on the A66, during the weekend of 7th to 9th December 1990, made the Team much more proactive in dealing with the press at any future incident and cemented the idea amongst a growing number of us that it was time for a change in name of the organisation from Fell Rescue to a Search and Rescue Team. Initially reports in the press regarding the blizzard made little if any mention of the Team. From a fundraising perspective, it became evident that the Team needed to raise its' own profile regarding search and rescue involvement and so I went along to the local newspaper, the Teesdale Mercury and spoke to Jim McTaggart at length. Jim had attended our AGMs and had always supported our work. The following report then appeared in the Wednesday addition of the Mercury;

Superb rescue work in storm

Teesdale Mercury

A magnificent job was done by fell rescue volunteers, police, council staff, RAF men and others to get over 200 travellers to safety in Teesdale during the weekend. But for their superb all-round effort some stranded people would have been in real danger of losing their lives and others would have been left in serious difficulties. While most of those saved were in vehicles blocked in by drifts on the A66 and other roads, a number of Dale residents were also helped while cut off in blizzards and power failures. There were scenes like war relief zones in the Bowes Moor Hotel, Bowes Village Hall and Witham Hall as victims of the sudden Arctic conditions, with ages ranging from 1 to over 80, were taken for shelter and food. Amongst the heroes were members of the Upper Teesdale and Weardale Fell Rescue Team, who were called out at 10pm on Friday and were on duty in shifts for nearly 48 hours. They insisted to the Mercury that their names should not be published as it was a Team effort, so we agreed to omit them, though feeling they all deserved a mention. Their first call was to a vehicle stranded above Crawleyside, Stanhope. A boy and girl were taken to safety from there before five of the Team's cross country skiers got to the scene. They found two men in a Range Rover with a trailer holding 27 beagles. They were persuaded to leave the dogs, though reluctant, and were taken to safety in Stanhope by 3 am. The dogs were collected later.

It was about 4 am by the time the rescuers reached Barnard Castle, where they were joined by some others and asked by police to go to Stainmore summit on the A66. Over the next four hours they skied and walked their way to the top, battling through fierce blizzards and huge drifts, and finding many people in cars and lorries. 'I've been on Cairngorm summits in blizzards but have known nothing worse than this.' The Team ensured that all stranded people were safe. An RAF helicopter arrived and took seven travellers to Bowes Moor Hotel around 11 am. It returned for five more, but a white-out near Valley Farm forced it to land and it could do no more. But the rescuers carried on, helping more stranded people to safety. By 7 pm they had checked 70 vehicles and ensured nobody was left in any of them. They spent the night in the hotel, along with over 100 rescued travellers. Next day, three of them flew in an RAF helicopter to Lunedale to look for other stranded people

Other members of the Team joined in with Tom Cole and his search dog, Mushie. They set up a control point at Mickleton, and later moved to make a search of Cotherstone Moor after a cry for help was reported. Nothing was found, and it was felt this might have been a farmer calling for his sheep. By this time on Sunday afternoon many of the rescuers were nearing exhaustion. But while some went home to sleep others answered another call for assistance and headed off for Woodland.

I was involved in a number of meetings with the police to look at lessons that could be learnt from the events of that weekend. I made the suggestion that barriers should be put in place on the A66, similar to those used on the high level routes in Scotland, that could be closed in the event of severe weather. I often recall the events of the weekend as I drive over to the Lakes, they are vividly etched in my memory.

There were a number of other successful small scale searches following that, and the methods of organising the Team to respond to these continued to give successful outcomes. In 1991 at an Extraordinary General Meeting the Association became the Teesdale and Weardale Search and Rescue Team. Jim McTaggart wrote an editorial in the Teesdale Mercury in December 1992 which crystallised the Team in this period, he said under the headline;

Dale is lucky to have a Team of rescuers turning out in all weathers

One of the unfortunate truths about the Search and Rescue Team which does a vast amount of valuable work in Teesdale, is that for much of the time it is taken for granted. In a way it's a victim of its own success, for it gets on with the task in such an efficient manner that it makes the whole operation seem exceedingly simple. Most of us tend to forget that the men and women who make up this dedicated outfit put an immense quantity of time and effort into training for the emergencies which crop up now and again. They also have to devote time to fundraising because essential equipment is very expensive. Their rigorous practice sessions usually take place at weekends when other people are relaxing, and are mostly at times of the year when the weather can be extremely nasty and dangerous. The point is that they have to learn to cope with appalling conditions because that is when visitors tend to get lost or injured in the wide open spaces. It is no use training only in sunny daylight and then having to turn out in darkness during a howling storm or in deep snow to get someone to safety. During the last serious wintry spell in Teesdale the rescuers gave magnificent service on a large scale. Considering that and other incidents over the years there are a number of people who owe their lives and good health to them.

Police officers who influenced the development of the Team

Each successful search demonstrated the capabilities of the Team to more Police Officers. There were a number who took a particular interest in the Team, and then later, when they moved to higher ranks, they were able to give us increasing amounts of support.

Bill Lippet, our long serving Police Liaison Officer in the 1980s, worked hard with Stan White to ensure that the means of contacting the Team was in place and callout lists were updated. Initially the police telephoned all the Team Members for a callout. We worked to change this to a cascade system, whereby only the Team Leader or Deputy Team Leader was called by the police, who then called non-active Team members, who then called out the remainder of the Team. This meant a much faster response, helping deal with previous criticism of the Team not being able to turn out in numbers quickly enough to effect efficient rescue.

Purchase of a cell phone, which needed a rucksack to carry around, and was only mobile if you were a weightlifter, was a first step to improving communications. The introduction of pagers, initially for the Team Leader and the Group Leaders, took us to a different level.

Another officer who had great influence was Inspector Dave Carroll. We first worked with Dave when a young fencing contractor became disorientated above the Stang Forest in a severe blizzard. Snow swept in late morning on a Thursday, his work mates managed to get initially to shelter, then to get off the moor to call for help when their colleague didn't join them. The callout came with just a few hours of daylight remaining.

We managed to assemble a good response to search the fence lines and the edge of the Stang Forest with 'Dog Des' covering some areas of open fell. As always in a search for missing person, there comes a point in the search when we would call in support from other Teams. This is always a difficult decision to reach for a Team Leader, as there are no hard and fast rules. You have to find the point at which your own Team has covered the most obvious likely areas where you expect the casualty to be and require wider coverage of an area. Sometimes once the other Teams are mobilised and en route, your own Team would find the casualty.

On this occasion, the point at which to bring in other Teams was quite early in the search because of the length of time the lad had been missing, his lack of emergency gear, the large area of ground in which he could be benighted and the severe conditions on the fell. The sectoring of the area, deployment of Teams, briefing sheets, and description of the missing young man had to be prepared and photocopied down at the Police Station in Barnard Castle ready for the first additional Team to arrive, whilst maintaining the flow of the search. The way in which the search progressed to its successful conclusion was a very good example of what we had been working towards. Dave Carroll was impressed when, after searching through the night, the young man, who had built himself a makeshift shelter to survive, was found by the Northumberland Team. Inspector Dave Carroll became our Police Liaison Officer and remained so when promoted to Chief Inspector. He was a man of great humour, always completely unruffled by any change in events; his calm, considered way of dealing with some traumatic situations was inspiring. Dave Carroll had a clear line as to what was 'police work' and what should be seen as decisions to be made by the Team Leader. He did everything he could to support the Team's work during incidents, when he could be contacted at any time of day or night if we had difficulty getting the resources we needed to undertake a task. Also in his role as Liaison Officer at Police Headquarters, he made a very significant contribution to the development of the Team and its relationship with Durham Constabulary.

Development of technical rescue methods

Countless sheep stuck on ledges or in quarries or old mine workings in both dales, High Force waterfall and, particularly, the rescue of a spaniel called 'Bully', made the public associate the Team with technical rescue. Ten days into the shooting season of 1990 a spaniel ran off from a party who were returning to their Land Rovers on Sharnberry Fell, and within a few seconds the dog had disappeared. One moment it was bouncing over heather, the next it had vanished! Hidden beneath the deep heather was a lead mine air shaft. As miners had tunnelled into the fell side following a lead vein on a 'level', they had dug shafts at intervals vertically upwards to allow air to get to the ever-longer tunnel. These were often lined with stone to prevent them from caving-in following heavy rain. The air shafts could be anything from about 10m to 50m or more in depth. Bully had bounced across the heather, which had parted, into a void about 10 to 15m deep. There are so many of these, the fells are often referred to as the 'hollow hills.'

Ian Findlay and others had, some years before, attempted the rescue of sheep from some of the more shallow shafts, and on at least one occasion, ended up being suspended from the front bucket of a local farmers' tractor. I believe Ian had been called by the farmer and told that if he didn't turn up with one of the 'fell rescue ropes' he would lower himself into the shaft. Foreseeing that hemp binder twine may not hold the weight of the rather beefy farmer, Ian had taken a Team climbing rope and then abseiled from the front bucket of the tractor into the shaft to recover the sheep.

Following this, and similar incidents, we tried to equip ourselves with various lengths of scaffolding poles to bridge a shaft. We had tried to build ourselves some sort of tripod using scaffolding clamps but in an earlier attempt had not quite got the physics right over one particularly wide shaft so that when loaded with a bag of cement the structure collapsed in on itself!

The shaft down which Bully had plummeted was a little over 1m wide and much overgrown with heather. We arrived with our selection of scaffold poles, cleared heather from around the shaft and to our great surprise felt we could hear the pining and whimpering of the dog. With the tripod/scaffold experience in our minds, we were able to simply lay two poles across the shaft. David Forster, who was the Team's most experienced caver/potholer, said he would 'give it a go'. Dave hung from the poles in a climbing harness then set up climbing tapes and a pulley with a second rope in the centre of the poles so that we could pull Bully out of the shaft. Dave abseiled down one rope and found that the shaft had a floor about 10m down on which Bully lay.

Dave tried not to put any weight on the 'floor' as often these were simply the build up of debris across a narrowing of the shaft that could collapse at any time. He grabbed Bully who proceeded to try to lick Dave to death - the kiss of life was normally from rescuer to casualty! Bully was put in a bag and hauled up to the surface to be reunited with his owner and the rest of the shooting party who were overjoyed with the return of the dog and took Bully to the safety of the Land Rovers…whilst a few of us stayed to make sure that Dave came out of the hole!

When I joined the Team, technical rescue equipment consisted of a steel stretcher designed by Peter Bell, an engineer who lived in Ambleside and was a member of the Langdale MR Team, a few climbing ropes of dubious origin, climbing and other assorted webbing tape, a low-stretch rope (which unlike a climbing rope, was designed to behave elastically absorbing some of the force built up when a climber falls) and some pulleys to erect an aerial ropeway.

It should be understood that rope rescue evolved from techniques used by climbers and mountaineers climbing vertical mountain and cliff faces, to effect the rescue of a fellow climber. These techniques have since been adapted by Members of Rescue Teams in the UK, USA and Europe for use in Technical Rescue.

A number of individual climbers, notably Hamish McKiness in the UK, an engineer and member of the Glencoe Mountain Rescue Team, had spent countless hours hanging on the end of a rope working out how simple pulley systems could be used to haul up an injured climber. Over time, others developed various devices for the controlled lowering of a stretcher down to a casualty.

There were a large number of ideas from many different sources as to the best way to set up, lower and then if necessary raise a stretcher back to the top of the cliff. In our case, that circumstance primarily applies to High Force. Team members attended a number of courses where different methods were advocated then tried to assemble a training programme to train Team members into the basics but with a 'Crag Group' of climbers who could set up the more complex systems. Crag training took place every two weeks during the summer with an annual spectacular for the visiting crowds at High Force waterfall.

Dave Forster was to bring all of this work together into a Crag Training Manual, which clearly structured the different levels of skill required of Crag Team Members. It was a model adopted by other Teams.

Our Crag Team practiced on all types of difficult terrain in the Dales and although it was thankfully a rare occurrence when someone had a mishap on steep or difficult ground, we were always successful in recovering a fallen casualty. To the credit of everyone, there was never any injury, even minor, sustained to any Crag Team Member in undertaking his or her task in very hazardous circumstances.

The late 1990s

When the Team moved away from just fell work, the rescues and searches were new territory. Methods long developed in training were put into action for the first time. Every rescue and every search always concluded with a de-brief to highlight lessons learnt or changes required that could make the outcome of a similar incident even more successful or effective. Sometimes, if all went well, the de-brief could last a few minutes but sometimes a whole evening would be taken up by a careful analysis of events.

In the late 1990s there were many rescues, including fell walkers and the vulnerable, dogs over cliffs or down mineshafts, sheep (more than 90 in total since the formation of the Team) and even a cow! A trawl of press cuttings on the Team's website will show that it was often the animals that gained the most publicity!

Casualties have been recovered after falling from mountain bikes and quad bikes - one homemade!

Team members were to use their first aid training to save life across the region, some even dealing with the most severe road traffic accidents on their way to and from training or a callout.

Searches ranged from a night of the most severe weather on Cross Fell, to river and town searches, often with the reality of the search being stranger than the fiction dreamed up in training scenarios. In one search, in a clearing in a wood near Barnard Castle over £13,000 worth of cannabis plants were found!

When I joined the Team in 1980 there were some years where there had been just 2 or 3 fell incidents, by the time I left to pursue my mountaineering ambitions in Europe, this had risen to over 40. The Team had come a long way, with many individuals making significant contributions to the development of the Team to meet the challenges and expectations. Inevitably in a brief history they are not all mentioned but to all of them and our Members today, the next casualty or missing person, owes their thanks.

Alan Best introduces search excercise 'looking for woollen dolls!'

The Pennines

'If the visitor isn't prepared, it's like a minefield'
- Ian Findlay 2009

Many thanks go to Ian Findlay for his contribution to this chapter. Ian has resided in Upper Teesdale for 35 years and was, for as many years, a Member of the Fell Rescue Team - later to become TWSMRT (Teesdale and Weardale Search and Mountain Rescue Team).

County Durham - the area covered by TWSMRT stretches from coastal areas overlooking the North Sea and climbs into the upland areas of the Northern England Pennines - 2,500 ft above sea level. The Pennine Way, the 'Backbone of England', continues for 280 miles, running from Derbyshire to Scotland, and is popular with walkers throughout the year. The northern part of the Pennine Way has some of the finest landscapes in the country and in 1988 was designated an Area of Outstanding Natural Beauty (AONB). At almost 2,000 square kilometers, it is the second largest of the 41 AONBs in the UK and one of the most remote and unspoilt places in England. The area holds great appeal to visitors with its high fells, heather moorland and many other natural attractions nestled amongst the vast countryside. As well as its AONB title, the North Pennines is also an UNESCO (United Nations Educational Scientific and Cultural Organisation) Geopark. In laymen's terms, a Geopark is an area designated for its geological and/or geomorphologic interest and it is the unique geology of the area created over millions of years that has sculptured the landscape we see today. Millions of years ago, the North Pennines was covered by a shallow tropical sea, and because of this, shellfish and corals gathered on the seabed and eventually hardened into limestone. The environment was made up of deserts and volcanoes, creating the intrusion of the famous Whin Sill 250 million years ago. The great Whin Sill is a hard, dark layer of rock known as dolerite created when molten lava pushed horizontally through the limestone and sandstone bands, and it heated the rock in the process. Once cooled and hardened underground it formed a flat sheet of rock known as a 'sill'. These numerous bands of rock have been exposed over millions of years through extremes of weather conditions - glacial flows, snow, rain and wind. One particular limestone band was half-baked and produced the famous sugar limestone that supports many unique arctic alpine plant species, which attract botanists worldwide to the area.

Flora

The intrusion of the Whin Sill played a significant part in establishing the unique flora found in and around Teesdale. The molten lava when coming into contact with the sandstone, shale and limestone had either a minimum effect or a dramatic change. Some sandstones changed colour, shale's baked and melmumby limestone was totally transformed from limestone to sugar limestone that formed a coarse, well-drained soil. Arctic alpine plants, which were wide spread in Britain pre ice age, disappeared as the climate became warmer except in isolated areas in upper Teesdale where conditions suited. The area has been called 'the

Valley of the ice flowers' and today, in early summer, rarities such alpine bisort, alpine rue, blue gentian and the unique Teesdale violet can be seen in the meadows in full bloom.

In 1967 however, the building of Cow Green Reservoir threatened the plants' habitat and brought about controversy as local conservationists got together to oppose the project. Cow Green reservoir is two miles long and its purpose was to serve the industries of Teesside, it took three years to build and was completed in 1971. Unfortunately, the conservationists lost their battle against the developers but thankfully only a tenth of the plants' habitat was destroyed and the remaining area became a National Nature Reserve.

The legend of Peg Powler

When Cow Green Reservoir was built, it was believed to have brought about the demise of a certain green creature that plagued the waters and bogs of the Teesdale area. According to English folklore, a green mermaid or hag with long hair, green skin and sharp teeth, known as 'Peg Powler', inhabited the River Tees. Grabbing the ankles of unsuspecting humans from the bank side, in particular naughty youngsters, she would drag her victims underwater and drown them. Her presence is indicated by a frothy substance on the surface of the water known as Peg Powlers suds. The myth originates from the 18th century when several children began to disappear without trace. Who knows if the building of the reservoir put an end to life of this gruesome hag, maybe it did. Nevertheless, I suppose you should always beware, and what a great excuse to keep your kids away from the water's edge.

Winter searching

The weather in Teesdale

The building of the Cow Green dam and all the publicity surrounding the project attracted the general public from all walks of life. A day out on a unique fell of international botanical importance, numerous walks, access road and car park at 1,600 ft above sea level was a must for many day visitors and school groups etc. During the 70s, an average of 70,000 plus were using the Cow Green area alone with even higher numbers in the lower dale. One ingredient not always taken into consideration by visitors, winter or summer, was the weather. Sunny mild conditions in lowland Durham can change dramatically once into the upland areas of the dales with a drop in temperature and deterioration of conditions. The winter periods brought fewer visitors, which meant fewer incidents. During the summer months there were many visitors inevitably leading to more incidents; few were serious but there were many minor ones. Unfortunately, a high proportion of these incidents came from schools and colleges etc where inadequate dress was the main problem. A code of conduct was agreed with the Education Authorities, which addressed many of these issues, and still works well today.

1970s also saw a change in the weather patterns up until the mid 70s. The winters were comparatively mild with snow and ice for short periods. That changed dramatically in 1976 with heavy snowfall that winter lasting 2-3 months. This pattern continued from 1976-1987. There were two incidents in 1976 that I recall, highlighting the extremes in weather conditions in this area. The first was during the summer months of July/August. It was a hot and dry summer and reports were coming in of a man who had collapsed on Mickle Fell (2, 600ft). A small team was called out and began the long walk onto the Fell. The collapsed man was found to be suffering from dehydration because of the heat. It was a long and difficult evacuation that took several hours. Fortunately, the outcome was successful. Following the hot summer came rainfall in September and October and snow in November, which lasted until March. One late evening in December a group arrived at Langdon Beck Youth Hostel. A man was reported missing en-route somewhere close to High Cup Nick. The Team were called out early in the morning and found that all upland roads were blocked by deep snow. The two groups deployed had to then follow the becks in very difficult conditions with deep snowdrifts and blizzards. It turned out to be a 14-hour day. The man was found safe and well because he had made himself a snow hole for the night.

These two incidents plus the numerous smaller ones during the 70s were undertaken with limited equipment - stretcher, casbag (a casualty bag is similar to a sleeping bag which is used during the transportation of casualties to keep them tightly wrapped and warm), basic first aid and only two field radios. The weather conditions in the upper Pennines and the Teesdale catchment area in particular has been likened to sea level in Iceland (Gordon Manly 1936). The main reason for this is the horseshoe shaped range of high fells surrounding the Tees basin - Mickle Fell 759m, Meldon Fell 767m, Knock Fell 750m, Green Dun Fell 868m, Little Dun Fell 842m, Yad Moss 746m, Fendrith Hill 696m and of course Cross Fell, the highest point of the Pennine Range, at 893m. This basin traps cold air producing a colder climate throughout the year. The arctic and alpine flora remnant from the last ice age are restricted to Upper Teesdale, which says a lot about the climatic conditions here. These same fells attract clouds producing a high rainfall, which supports two major rivers - the Tees and the South Tyne.

The Upper dales differ in their topography. Baldersdale, Lowedale and Weardale are 'V' shaped dales with human habitants and farming in the lower reaches. Teesdale however, is 'U' shaped and settlements in this dale are at a much higher altitude than other dales. Farming in the upper dales is difficult; the growing season is short (mid May - late September) so livestock farming is the only option. Arable crops are a non-starter. The weather conditions control the farming year, which makes for a very hard life for these tough dales folk.

Its not all doom and gloom, as early March sees the return of the Waders (Lapwing, Redshank, Snipe, Curlew and Golden Plover) back for the breeding season and in full song. Later, pastures and hay meadows are full of colour with the numerous flora species. A short season but what a show. The dales folk, birds and flora have adapted to these conditions and learn to live with the dramatic change in weather that can occur.

Cross Fell

At 2,930 ft, Cross Fell is the highest point of the Pennines and steeped in mythical history. Overlooking the Eden Valley, on clear days you see views of the mountains of the Lake District and, on the Northern side, you can see as far as the Solway Firth and southern parts of the uplands of Scotland. It's also where the River Tees begins its journey to the North Sea as no more than a trickle. There are many theories as to how Cross Fell got its name but in ancient times it was known as Fiend's Fell by locals and believed to be haunted by evil spirits. During a visit by St Paulinus, a Christian missionary, a mass was held on the peak and a cross erected to drive out the demons and mark the exorcism in the 7th century. However many locals believe this exorcism was unsuccessful and that one demon remains, disguising itself as a fierce wind known as the Helm Wind. The Helm Wind, a northeasterly wind that blows down the southwest slope of the Cross Fell escarpment, is the only named wind in the British Isles and its gusts are often described and likened to that of a hurricane. This phenomenon occurs more frequently during the summer months and can last for several days. Certainly not ideal walking conditions. To walk the 11 miles of the escarpment for 6 -7 hours is tough and challenging at the best of times and should only be attempted when the weather is clear and you are equipped with a map and compass.

Treating a casualty inside a group shelter

Industry

The North Pennines were a hive of industry during the 18th and 19th centuries and the area is steeped in lead mining history which dates right back to the 1300s. It began on a very small scale in Cumbria, Weardale and Nenthead before spreading into Teesdale in the 1700s. It was a London based lead company that increased the population in Teesdale at this time, employing thousands of men and boys with families being brought in from Derbyshire and Cornwall. Six of those families remain in the area today. They also built houses, schools, libraries, and were the first company to introduce a five-day week. The landscape is now dotted with disused shafts and mine levels which, for the unwary, can be very dangerous. The hard lives these people led is reflected in a commemorative local song dating back to the 1860s and credited to Thomas Raine, its' title is 'Four Pence a Day,'

The ore is waiting in the tub, the snow's upon the fells

Canny folk are sleeping yet, but lead is ret to sell,

Come me little washer lad, come lets away

We're bound down for slavery for four pence a day,

Its early in the morning, we rise at five o' clock

And the little slaves come to the door to knock knock knock

Come me little washer lad, come lets away

Its very hard to work for four pence a day

My father was a miner, he worked down in the town

Twas hard work and poverty that always kept him down

He aimed for me to go to school but brass he couldn't pay,

So I had to go to the washing rake for four pence a day.

My mother rises out of bed with tears on her cheeks

Puts my wallet on her shoulder which has come to serve a week

It often fills her great big heart when she unto me say

I never thought thou would have worked for four pence a day

Four pence a day, me lad, and very hard to work

And never a pleasant look from a gruffy looking 'Turk'

His conscience it may fall and his heart may give away

Then he'll raise our wages to nine pence a day

For those with an interest in this industrial history, a visit to Killhope Museum or Nenthead Mines will provide the answers in a safe environment.

Industrial heritage of the North Pennines

The Teesdale honey pots

Upper Teesdale is home to three dramatic waterfalls, one of which is the largest in England. High Force waterfall, situated in Forest-in-Teesdale on the Raby Estate, is probably the most visited tourist attraction in the area with thousands flocking every year, especially during the summer months. Just a pleasant woodland walk of 1/3 of a mile will lead you to this breathtaking spectacle and it is here where you can also see a fine example of the famous Whin Sill outcrop as the Tees River dramatically drops 70ft into the plunge pool below. High Force should always be treated with respect and during TWSMRT's 40 years of history, the Team have attended numerous incidents that have occurred here, from evacuating casualties with fractured ankles to sadly dealing with fatalities. In 1994, following the death of a North-East man, discussions took place with the local Council to decide if anything more could be done to make the area a safer place for visitors. It was even suggested to block it off completely to the public. Fortunately that never happened, but Councillor Ken Saxby, also a member of TWSMRT, had this to say at the meeting, 'Notices had been put up warning visitors to beware of the dangers and not go too near the edge. Some people still went onto the centre rocks and stood near the end to take photographs. I doubt if any further warning signs would have any impact, as people would not pay any heed to them'. Sadly, this is true so it is little wonder the Team often do their high line rope rescue training here.

Further down river is Low Force Waterfall, the second of Teesdale's 'honey pots' and another popular spot for day visitors. Although not as intensely dramatic as High Force, Low Force has a picturesque beauty that is just as impressive and attractive but equally as dangerous if its visitors do not take caution. Below the waterfall is the Wynch Bridge, which was erected in 1820 so the miners could reach the mines at Middleton from Holwick (The Team can be spotted here whilst undertaking swift water training).

Situated below Cow Green Dam in the upper reaches of Teesdale, before the river reaches High and Low Force, is Cauldron Snout, which is an impressive collection of waterfalls and at 200 yards long, is said to be England's longest waterfall. It also claims the title of England's highest waterfall as it measures 200ft vertically from the first cataract to the last. It is a popular place, proving the two-mile walk from the car park at Cow Green is well worth it to take in the view. It is also another spot that is not without incident. Cauldron Snout has brought about a fair few callouts for the Team, however amongst them all there is a memorable one for Ian Findlay.

A fall to see a fall

The Team were called out to attend to a lady with a broken ankle. At the scene, first aid was administered and the lady was placed on a stretcher ready for the carry out over steep ground eastside of Cauldron Snout. The lady, with her companion, had walked from Widdy Bank Farm to see Cauldron Snout waterfall. The lady with the broken ankle had last seen the waterfall 50 years previously and was disappointed at having come so far to miss it. The Team decided they would take her to see the falls from the stretcher. On reaching high ground, the stretcher was lowered then raised at the head end to enable her to have a spectacular view of the falls. Several photographs later and a reasonably happy lady was taken to the waiting ambulance to head off to the hospital.

Upland areas, even on sunny days, need to be treated with respect. Remember the higher you walk or climb, the lower the temperature. Enjoy the spectacular landscape and natural attractions in all its seasons; but always with a healthy respect for the terrain and its weather.

Trig point and cairn in the North Pennines

Base, Training and Equipment

Base

'We were founded 30 years ago and in all that time we have not had a permanent base. We have decided to launch an appeal to build a permanent base - once and for all.'
-Steve Owers, 1999, Press officer (TWSMRT)

A wooden hut, a collection of garages and a number of pubs are amongst the places the Team have had to use as a base and for training purposes, over the last 40 years. Back in the very early days of the fledgling Team, the newly dedicated bunch of volunteers set to work to build themselves their first ever base situated behind the High Force Hotel on a piece of land donated by the Raby Estate. Of course, to call it anything other than what is was would be dressing it up somewhat, because it was just simply a wooden hut. Materials had been donated by a local business and members spent their free time and weekends erecting it. Basic, yes, but still home to the Team and serving its purpose for some 30 years up until the late nineties. It certainly says something about the guys' nifty workmanship for it to be standing that length of time, the only thing to bring it down, unfortunately, was a tree, when it fell on the roof shortly after the Team vacated it.

The hut had room for the Team's Land Rover and a few shelves on the walls for storage, which meant that either the equipment officer or Team members themselves, had to take most of the kit home. To put into perspective just how small it was, the hut had an office area, which held at a push, only 10 people. Take into account how many actual members were on the Team and you can see why it was impossible for them all to congregate into such a small space without the place literally bursting at the seams, which is why training and meetings took place at other various locations. The most regular of places were the Wheatsheaf Inn at Staindrop, Staindrop Comprehensive School and Bishop Auckland Police Station Social Club. Logistically it wasn't ideal, but nonetheless the Team continued to run efficiently and effectively. As the Team developed and became more diverse in its' role as a rescue service, it became more practical to move on to different premises so it was around 1998 when it moved into a collection of garages rented from Teesdale District Council at Barnard Castle. Again, it still only offered a limited amount of office space, with housing for two vehicles so that training still had to continue at the locations mentioned earlier. Towards the end of the lease period for the garages, Durham Police Authority approached the Team offering a piece of land they had available for lease adjacent to Barnard Castle Police Station. The rent was low, the location was suitable, it was an offer the Team couldn't refuse, however there was one slight problem, which was that there was no money to fund a new building.

Mountain Rescue is a registered charity, are totally self sufficient and rely heavily on donations, as the only way it survives as a part of the emergency services. It is the umbrella organisation under which the Team operates.

The Team, also a registered charity, did not have thousands of pounds to build new headquarters. It was never going to be as simple as that. A plan was needed how to raise the money, if it was to be up and running in their new home by 2001.

Base appeal 2001

The estimated cost of the project was in the region of £150,000; £25,000 covered equipment and training costs, which the Team Members planned to raise themselves and the remaining £125,000 was for the building itself. An application was made for lottery funding. This was a serious amount of money, so it was decided that Base Appeal 2001 should be launched. Chris Scott, Team treasurer, coordinated the project, whilst Alan Best had the unenviable responsibility of motivating the Team into what appeared at the time as a mammoth task.

Fundraising began on a huge scale and was underway by Easter 1999. To mark the launch of the Appeal, the first event was a coast-to-coast cycle ride beginning at Whitehaven. Amongst other events taking place, the Team came up with the idea of the 'Buy a Brick Appeal'. The response was excellent with 155 people or companies buying bricks, although, rumour has it that Chris Scott allegedly employed a friend to 'go round and persuade people'.

Persuaded or not, with the help of Chris' friend £350 was raised from his efforts and by way of a thank you, sponsors who made a donation received their own Buy a Brick Appeal certificate signed by Alan Best and their names were put onto the Roll of Honour, which is on display in the Base today.

The appeal also had a positive effect by increasing their number of associate members - of the 155 sponsors, 69 became associate members, bringing the total to around 80. The Team secured lottery funding, injecting £125,000 into the project, ensuring building works finally began in September 2000.

By the time fundraising was complete, the Team's efforts had well exceeded the original £25,000 they set out to attain. Stan White, Team Secretary at the time, had this to say in a newsletter following completion of the appeal, 'For most fundraising events, you can almost name the names of those who are going to turn up on the day; it's always been like that and probably always will be so. However, when the idea of the Rescue Centre was first mooted, it seemed to grab the imagination of everybody and coupled with Alan's determination this served to see the project through to the magnificent results we have today.'

So, tucked neatly behind Barnard Castle Police Station now stands what is undoubtedly the Team's biggest and proudest achievement to date. After years in the planning, unrelenting fundraising and excellent teamwork, Lord Barnard officially opened the new purpose built Rescue Centre on March 31st 2001, turning the dream into a well-deserved reality. The new Base boasts a garage for the Team's two vehicles and trailer; it also contains the crag rescue training (climbing) wall and a platform for shaft rescue training. Adjoining this is a drying room with a high capacity dehumidifier and electric heater for equipment if it is wet or damp. The

Base also includes a control room with an archive store, kitchen area, and disabled toilet facilities. There is a large meeting and presentation area upstairs equipped with a power point computer system, an array of audio-visual equipment including video projection as well as ample storage and maintenance areas for all of the Teams' kit.

Training

In the early days of the rescue service, training was fairly limited as the Team Members relied primarily on their own knowledge and supplementary information given to them by farmers and gamekeepers who knew their local areas well. The rescuers had limited first-aid equipment and could not afford two-way radio equipment for their operations.

As the Fell Rescue Team established itself, training exercises involved more advanced equipment and vehicles. In 1980, two dozen members took part in an exercise in an RAF Sea King helicopter for the first time. The volunteers were transported across the countryside with their stretchers and rescue equipment, stopping at Coldberry, Goldsborough and Harwood to aid exercise 'victims.' Such support, although relatively uncommon in real rescues, is now an essential part of the working knowledge of the Team; such has been the development of the organisation over the last forty years.

Although this is a voluntary service, members of the Team are well trained, qualified and equipped to deal with an emergency, employing similar principles adopted by the Emergency Services. The Team can therefore operate either relatively independently, or alongside the other emergency services.

Base Opening Day - Vehicle now replaced

An example of this occurred during a callout in the Easington Colliery area of County Durham where TWSMRT were first responders after being contacted by the Police and coordinated the search for a missing middle-aged man. The Team and the Police searched the area in heavy rain overnight.

Team Leader, David Bartles-Smith, requested assistance from neighbouring MR Teams, which included Northumberland, Swaledale and Cleveland, when the man still had not been found in the morning.

For those who may not be familiar with Easington Colliery, it is a village located near the North East Coast, so Team Leader David, also requested assistance from the Coastguard and the RNLI. The man was later found by a stream south of Easington, airlifted to a waiting ambulance, and taken to hospital. A successful operation.

Approximately 50 volunteers were out over the weekend working with the Police, the Police helicopter and the ambulance service. TWSMRT were heavily involved in the coordination of the operation, proving volunteers are an invaluable and respected asset.

On joining the Team, it is expected that successful applicants have relevant hill experience and are willing and available to undertake the demands of probationary training. The probationary period lasts for 12 months and recruits are not eligible for a callout unless they have completed and passed the relevant training required of them. There are twelve sections in the training logbook:

- Rescue Organisations
- Search Methods
- Fell craft and Navigation
- Rescue Centre and Vehicles
- Communications and Radio Procedure
- Casualty Care
- Rope Rescue
- Crag Training
- Air Support
- Crashed Aircraft
- Water
- River Rescue

The skills and knowledge in each section are divided into three categories, Foundation, Intermediate and Advanced.

It is expected that all Team Members, through their own training programme, will acquire and maintain the skills and knowledge for the Foundation level in each section. A probationary Member must therefore complete all of this, prior to assessment for full Team Membership.

The competencies at the Intermediate level, lead on from the Foundation level and represent what Team Members should know and work towards.

At the Advanced level, which some Team Members could acquire at various competencies, specialist skills and knowledge is gained, such as the Advanced Casualty Carer and Technical Rope Rescue.

The criteria can be met by way of worksheets, practical exercises, videos, books and power point presentations for example. Ongoing training is vital, and the Team trains fortnightly on a weekday evening, often at the Base, where it is warm and dry. However, it is in the harsh, demanding conditions of the North Pennines that the Team usually holds its' monthly exercises.

Whilst the Team is out training on the fells, you could certainly feel quite sorry for them, but spare a thought for the volunteer, who has offered to be the exercise 'body.' A 'body' is a casualty with fictitious injuries – where possible someone unfamiliar to the Team, such as an Associate Member - who places and conceals themselves in a remote area, before waiting for the team to find them, which could be many hours later.

Most have said it was a good experience and our thanks go to all those that have helped improve the Team skills of searching, casualty care and evacuation.

First year as a team member

Paul Allison completed his probationary period in March 2008; he very kindly offered to tell all about his time (in his own words) as a probationary Member and why he joined TWSMRT.

Part One
February 1992

We hadn't picked a great week for our winter break. In those days, we both worked in rope access (think steeple jacking but without the pipes, flat caps and barge ropes) and still thought that any time off work must involve climbing stuff. We'd driven around the highlands trying to pick off reasonably sensible routes in deteriorating conditions. Grade IVs had been the order of the week and we'd hit Craig Meagaidh, the Ben, and Glencoe and now found ourselves in the car park under Buachaille Etive Mor.

The brew's on and we extricate ourselves from our pits, rummaging around to find grub, clothes and gear amongst the build up of detritus inevitable in a car that's been our home for the last few days. It takes longer than normal to get going, but by fiveish we're on our way, trudging through the snow heading for Crowberry Ridge. After a few hundred yards, we grind to a halt. Everything feels wrong; there's no bite in the snow, no crunchy steps, no clouds of breath, we're not freezing cold stamping around when we stop.

"Too warm?"

"Yep."

"Let's go."

We retrace our steps, crossing with other groups heading in to the crag; all grown ups, none of our business. Back to the car, half in pits, radio on, brew on, a wee dram, a couple of tabs each, and a long snooze. Mid morning and we're considering the future; today's a dead loss; the pub will be open by eleven and twelve hours in the bar seems a good option. The car's fogged up. We wipe off the condensation once in a while

Current Control Vehicle and now replaced Land Rover

and peer out at the day; the only colour we've seen since dawn is grey and it doesn't seem to be improving. We're roused from warm thoughts of the pub by a sudden hammering on the roof and I wind down the window. Holy Moly! It's MacInnes; winter climbing guru, inventor of the Terradactyl, leader of Glencoe Mountain Rescue Team and perhaps the most Scottish looking person ever. He glares in at us and demands,

"Are you boys any good?"

We look at each other and mutter something clever about being good enough to have stopped in the car park today.

"Come on then."

We're confused, but we get out of the car. MacInnes has arrived in a blue panel van with a huge searchlight on the roof.

"Expecting the Luftwaffe are we?"

He has no time for smart arse Sassenachs,

"Get your gear and take these."

We are handed what appears to be two sets of tent poles. More lads arrive and we get the gist of what is happening. The team's been out for three days straight, on one job after another. They're all knackered. Most of them are at home in bed. They've just had another callout and, short of manpower, they are reduced to co-opting English idiots found languishing in the car park. More team members are on their way, but we set off in a small group pretty much immediately. On the way in, we pick up more of the story. Two climbers were avalanched on the Buachaille this morning, one is missing and, this is the thing, they all know the lad. The walk in is subdued and quiet.

The avalanche debris is obvious but not huge; it's confined to a shallow gully below the steep central section of the crag. Unlucky.

We're directed to form a close order line of search. Out come the tent poles/avalanche probes and it isn't very long at all before he's found and dug out. More team members arrive. We step back; he wasn't our mate and it's obvious we aren't part of this anymore. We head down and don't stop until we're snug in front of fire in the public bar of the Kings House.

Part 2
April 2006

For the life of me, I can't remember what made me think of joining the Teesdale and Weardale Mountain Search and Rescue Team. Maybe it was the way the name trips so easily off the tongue. Anyway, I did think of it and it seemed like a good idea, why? Well, I don't know for sure... Was it volunteering my rather rusty mountaineering skills to bring aid and succour to stranded hill walkers trapped in a blizzard high on the North Pennines?

Nope.

Being one of Tony Blair's active citizens helping to maintain a cohesive society by giving something back?

No, not that either.

Playing 'cowboys and injuns' in the hills with the possibility of damsels in distress? Hello!

So, I sent an email in asking how to join. I was told that I was too late for this year's intake and I should apply next year to join the "C list" (whatever that might be). The "C list" hmmm, alphabetically that must be pretty damn close to being the best list to be on. It's February 2007 and I get an invite to an open evening at the base in Barnard Castle. I go along and cripes, there's a lot of people here. Someone says that 150 people have expressed an interest. As I'm chatting to people, I realise that there are some right weirdo's wandering around. I know that one of my many faults is that I think that everyone in the world is strange apart from me, but even so, there are some proper will-be-on-the-news-one-day fruit-loop-peddlers here.

This evening is supposed to inform us of the work of the team, the range of incidents and the geographic spread and to ensure that we fully understand the commitment necessary. I establish that both playing cowboys and injuns and damsels in distress feature heavily and I make my mind up to apply to join the alphabetically exalted "C List."

I receive a three-page application form in the post. A form? I have to set out my experience of mountaineering and supply the names and addresses of two referees.

It's what applying for a job must be like.

So, I fill it in and don't tell any lies at all. Even, both referees are real people. I get accepted. Yippee, on the "C List", err not quite.

I'm allowed to attend the first hill test day, my performance on which will determine whether I am allowed to attend the second hill test day, and if I pass that then I get to join the "C List."

What the hell happened to, "Are you boys any good?"

I don't know how many people returned application forms. Eighteen are invited to the first hill test day. It's a lovely sunny March day out on the hills between Baldersdale and the A66. We're allocated in groups to an experienced member of the Team. We go for a walk and are assessed on hill craft, fitness, navigation and probably affability and common sense. It seems straightforward, but only twelve are invited to join the team; so, I get to join the "C List".

Of course, as it turns out, there are only three lists in the pile, and the other two are the "A list" and the "B list", making "C list" the bottom one. Bugger.

So, here we are, February 2007 and we have a year's training ahead of us before we're allowed out to play on jobs. We have to attend 5 weekend exercises, 5 Wednesday evening sessions and an overnight exercise. I go to five weekends and enjoy them all. They are mainly days out in the West Durham hills playing hide and seek. Stand outs are the first one on the fells at Snowhope in proper winter conditions, a November day / night / day above Teesdale and a tramp around Consett, Houndsgill and Derwent Reservoir.

I fit in a lot of Wednesday training nights, usually fun, usually interesting and a lot is learned, forgotten, learned again and partially retained.

Overall, the training days and nights allow us to learn the bare essentials of fell search and rescue, give us time and room to practice these things and provide an environment in which we get to know each other better and how the team operates.

After a year, we come to our assessment. There is a written paper. We do it in our own time. It mainly serves to remind me how many of the details of the Team operations I do not know.

The assessment proper is a day and a night on the hill. The day is spent demonstrating our knowledge of and familiarity with "Control" (a pimped Iveco panel van). The comedy awning takes us by surprise, but we get the better of it in the end; no canvas based life form's going to outwit us thank you very much.

The night navigation test involves finding a series of exact map locations on the fell. We're in a group of four, Dave and me under scrutiny from Tom and Danny. All goes swimmingly on the navigation front, but Dave is suffering with a really bad cough. We pause. Dave is coughing his guts ups. Dave sounds like he's dying; uh oh, apparently he is. Medic! Dave goes off to hospital, but has done enough.

In another group, Tony gets a bad eye and is also sent to hospital. We know he's a scaredy-cat-afraid-of-the-dark-girl-pants, so are not too surprised that's he's bottled it (alternative explanation; Tony ends up in hospital for two days and two months of treatment because his eye was exploding). Then we get our heads down in bivi bags for a few hours.

In the morning, I'm told that for some fellow assessmentees a sleepless night was made worse by the sound of my snoring; it makes me feel warm inside.

All of us that are out that night pass and join the team as full Members. Passing the final assessment and joining the Team feels like the beginning of something, not the end. Six months later, I still have the remains of an outsider's sense of perspective about the Team, but I know it won't be long before it's completely disappeared.

So before it does, any pearls of wisdom from a year being on the "C List" and six months in the team. No, but maybe some things that might pass as thoughts.

The team has highly skilled Members and highly developed systems. In this sense, it is an elite group, but somehow it manages to avoid the silliness typical of such groups. We formed quick friendships with our fellow "C Listers", but are also made to feel part of the Team by long standing Members a long time before we deserve to be. The Team could give lessons on how to be elite without being elitist.

Apparently, Mountain Rescue has the highest divorce rate of the emergency services. I'm not surprised. As far as better halves are concerned, whether they've bought the line about a deep personal voluntary commitment to saving lives in remote areas, or they've seen through us and cottoned on the whole cowboys and injuns for grown ups thing, the up side for them is hard to see. I suppose it gets us out of the house. Alongside developing our core fell search and rescue skills, the Team offers opportunities for us to develop more and more technical expertise in several specific areas, so much so that pressure of time leads us to de facto specialisation.

The Youth Team using the indoor climbing facility at the Base. 'The Everest Challenge Fundraiser'

My background lends itself to rope rescue work. Others favour water based search and rescue, casualty care, dogs, search management, etc. Some have the time and motivation to work on most or all of these. Technical specialisation within the Team comes with potential risk to overall Team cohesion. Training to improve technical expertise is usually done in a small group; this is effective for individuals and helps develop teamwork and team spirit. The trick is to recognise the potential for a split team inherent in this; and avoid it.

So, we're on the "A List". We know we still know nothing. We go on callouts. We start to do additional training and develop special powers of search, casualty care, water and crag. But first things first, where are the new "C List" to pick on? Schadenfreude is an underrated pastime. What do you mean we're not recruiting this year? Rubbish!

Equipment

Issue and receipt book,	1		3	6		3	6
					280	1	3
Other proposals.							
Oversuits,lightweight, Helly Hensen	16	11	3	6	178	16	0
1" to 1 mile maps,Teesdale,Sheet 84.	6		6	6	1	19	0
Handtorches,	6		15	0	4	10	0
Whistles,	6		4	6	1	7	0
Bamboo canes, 3 ft. 100per bundle,	2		16	5	1	12	10
Vehicle inspection lamp,	1	1	10	0	1	10	0
Rucksacks, Karrimor Aiguille,	2		5	0	10	0	0
Jack and tools for landrover.	say		3	0	0	3	0	0
					£ 48 2	16	0

Equipment proposed by sub-committee 1 Nov 68

The above list of proposed equipment was taken from the minutes of a meeting held way back in 1968 just weeks following the official formation of the Rescue Team. This small example illustrates just how far the Team has come in terms of development and equipment over the last forty years. However, many of the basics are still the same - maps, compass, a head torch, whistles, a rucksack or backpack, all of which today's Members are expected to carry with them, amongst other things, as part of their personal kit. The advancement of technology has meant the Team has acquired some seriously sophisticated pieces of equipment, enabling them to undertake some more complex rescues. It is impossible to list every item of kit in this book, so the aim of this section is to give you an overview of key equipment currently in use.

Team photograph at the opening of the Base 2001

Equipment used in casualty evacuation

The Team currently employs four types of stretchers for use in casualty evacuations, the 'Bell', the 'Scoop', the 'Neil Robertson' and the 'Ferno'. The type of stretcher used depends on the nature of the rescue, taking factors into account such as terrain, casualty injuries and the distance the casualty needs transporting.

The first is the Neil Robertson stretcher, which was adapted in the 1900s, designed for use in confined spaces such as caves and mines, and is useful for vertical hauls and lowers into shafts and potholes. It is hardwearing and light in order for it to be manoeuvred through tight cave passages. It's made of wood and canvas but originally it was handmade, using bamboos. The stretchers first official title was quite a lengthy one, known, as a 'Hammock for hoisting wounded men from stokeholds and for use in ships whose Ash Hoists are 2ft. 6 in. diameter.'

Next is the Bell stretcher, which was adapted from the Thomas stretcher. In the 1960s, Peter Bell from Keswick MRT had the idea of halving the Thomas stretcher for easy storage and to enable quick and easy transport to the casualty site. The two halves connect together and can be carried or slid over snow or grass. It has also been used in steep ground and crag rescue situations. The Bell stretcher is widely popular, used by many rescue teams, and is TWSMRT's primary stretcher.

The Scoop stretcher is rarely ever used on its' own, but as it is a split construction, it can be assembled around casualties prior to lifting them onto the Vacuum Mat; very useful for casualties suffering from back injuries.

The Ferno stretcher is primarily used for crag rescue as it is very strong and lightweight but is not convenient to transport patients any significant distance.

Like all things regarding health and safety, there are procedures involved when lifting stretchers and casualties. Here are the true, if gruesome, consequences of getting it wrong. This occurred when the Team discovered a very badly decomposing body.

Once the appropriate scene of crime was completed, the Team then had to recover the body to the nearest road. Each Team Member took up position either side of the body and got as secure a grip as possible. Next, they were called to lift on the count of three. One Team Member took this to mean on the actual three whilst everyone else thought it was three and then lift. On three, the one at the head end stood up, holding the head but unfortunately, none of the other Team Members had moved.

The bits were reunited later, but just imagine doing the same with a live casualty with a broken neck - it could have fatal consequences. Lessons were learnt that day.

There are three key pieces of equipment used in conjunction with the Bell stretcher to protect the casualty and promote recovery: Casualty Bag (CAS-Bag), Head Blocks, and the Vacuum Mattress (Vac-Matt).

The CAS-Bag is an essential piece of equipment for 99% of all live casualty evacuations. The bag protects the casualty from the elements, has a windproof/water resistant outer, and is insulated inside with a fibre pile inner. It also has a series of handles so that it can lift on/off the stretcher. Other features are a see-through panel for casualty information and reversible zips to give access to the casualty without uncovering them completely.

Head blocks are used to stabilise the head where a spinal injury is suspected. The Vac-Matt is a full body splint that shapes to the contours of an injured person. The mattress contains thousands of small beads and by sucking out the air with a vacuum pump, the mattress becomes rigid.

Vehicles

'In August 1988, the unthinkable happened when the Fell Rescue Team was "relieved" of its Land Rover Ambulance by an unknown thief. Unthinkable indeed - who would want to steal a vehicle which bore the words "AMBULANCE" and "RESCUE" and was obviously an emergency vehicle?'
- Stan White (Hon. Secretary) 1990

Shamelessly someone stole the rescue vehicle from outside a member's house in Shildon. The Team thought it would be recovered or found burnt out, but puzzlingly there was never any trace of the vehicle or its contents. Many years later, the mystery was solved - we were informed that it had turned up in Africa . It was a blow to an organisation that saves lives voluntarily, acquiring things like vehicles and equipment through the hard work of raising their own funds. To steal a lifeline like that is incomprehensible and, consequently, the Team realised how limiting one vehicle could be, but they also discovered how resourceful they had to be.

During one particular callout involving Scarborough MRT, Stan White noticed they had a new Land Rover and after speaking with one of their Team Members, Stan discovered they had raised the cash themselves through various fundraising efforts over an 18-month period. This led to him having the fanciful idea of doing the same. The idea came up for discussion during the next Committee meeting and the amount they were looking at was £10,000. Stan threw himself into the project, expecting money to trickle in but within weeks the Team's President, Lord Barnard, donated a generous amount, getting things really moving. Following that, the Team then received another magnificent cheque from Her Majesty Queen Elizabeth the Queen Mother, who took a particular interest in all things concerning Teesdale due to her Strathmore family ties.

By September 1989, the amount raised was £11,000 pounds enabling the team to purchase a white, long-wheelbase Land Rover.

The team today operates two purpose built vehicles. The first is the Control vehicle (Control) which is based on an Iveco van; it has a side door entry to the control area, which has seating for two controllers and another five personnel. The vehicle is equipped with a range of radios for communication with search groups, helicopters, other Teams and the Police. A computer system is on board allowing for logging of all information collected during a search and GPS tracking of search groups.

An additional flat panel display allows the search controllers to view the log as well as a computerised map of the search area supplied by the police.

There is a main storage area at the back of the vehicle, which is large enough to accommodate a generator, a selection of search, rescue, medical and climbing equipment.

There is vanex shelter fitted to one side, providing a secure area for Team briefings.

As an ambulance, it is also used for transporting casualties.

The second vehicle is affectionately named 'Stan's Van', in recognition of the 25 years of service given to Mountain Rescue by the aforementioned Stan White, who sadly died in 2002 and who was, for many years, the Team's Secretary.

Stan's Van is a Land Rover Td5 110 Station Wagon (Mobile), and its' main use is to transport groups to the search area. It has seating for the driver and six passengers. The radio fit is similar to that in Control and if necessary it is sometimes used to control a second search operation.

Mobile carries a variety of equipment similar to Control both in the rear of the vehicle and in a roof box. Again, the vehicle can quickly be configured to carry a casualty on a full-length stretcher for transporting either to hospital or from rough terrain to a tarmac road for handover to an NHS ambulance.

As with all Team equipment, a great deal of fundraising was required to purchase both these vehicles and, indeed, other kit, and the Team gratefully acknowledges the generosity of all those who donate money.

www.twsrt.org

MOUNTAIN RESCUE COUNCIL · ENGLAND & WALES

DBS in the Current Control Vehicle

The Team Today

Role of the Team Leader - David Bartles-Smith (DBS)

The Team Leader (TL) role encompasses two distinct functions, operational and business. The role as Chair of the Trustees that govern the charity is a complex role, bringing together all the functions that enable the organisation to provide the service it delivers. This includes chairing a management committee and covers all areas from training, networking and accountancy, to maintenance of the Base and the vehicles. The Team delegates many of these tasks to individual officers but the role of the Chair is to steer and guide the management committee towards the long-term goals of the Team. This role can be very involved and the growth of the organisation over the past few years has necessitated a very business-like approach to this. Not only do we have to maintain and support our operational status but this has also to be managed in a way that is both accountable and compliant with Charity Commission guidelines.

The other distinct role as operational lead for the Team is the role that readers will be perhaps more aware of. Any search and rescue operation requires leadership and the Team operates a distinct command structure. The Team Leader will have ultimate responsibility for the decision-making on strategy and implementation. Usually the call from the Police will be taken by the TL, who will have to make a decision about the most appropriate response. This could be to initiate an immediate callout or to put the Team on standby. The TL is in direct contact with the Police and once a callout is 'paged' a command structure is then initiated. This involves the three Deputies and can also draw on input from the Teams' leads on casualty care, search dogs, technical rescue and water search and rescue.

A rendezvous (RV) point is established and Team members meet at this point. Some pick up the Team vehicles and undertake a range of other predetermined tasks. Very soon, the Team resources are in place and throughout this, the TL has been developing the initial response strategy. This can vary from initial hasty searches to immediate assistance at a known casualty site.

After this first phase, and once actions are in place, the TL will then head up the now formed Command Team. Usually this will comprise of at least four people. This group decides on strategy, implements the plan, records the outcomes and provides the operational link to the Police and other agencies that may be involved. Sometimes the TL will have to give media interviews, both live and recorded.

Perhaps the biggest attraction in the role is the unpredictable nature. One moment I can be at work or home and the next engaged in a major incident - dealing with a crisis, finding a strategy and attending interviews of families and dealing with the media. All in all a very complex role that draws upon a range of knowledge and skills. It is essentially full time, in that there are always tasks that need attention too!

Search and management

'Search is the classic mystery. You are looking for the needle in a very big haystack. In the case of the High Pennines the haystack is made up of areas of deep heather, peat bogs, deep cuttings, beck's and rivers which, in full spate, become powerful raging torrents as well as perhaps forest and countless air shafts and levels.'
-Alan Best

Managing a search

The Team not only searches for lost hill walkers but has also in recent years become more involved in searches for people missing through all areas of County Durham and indeed beyond. Vulnerable missing people are now a core part of our work and a wealth of theory now supports how we manage these searches. The responsibility for anyone reported missing is with the Police and after assessment of the vulnerability of the missing person it may be determined that a search needs to take place as concern is high. This will include the elderly, children, people who are despondent and such groups as Alzheimer's sufferers.

The search will be lead by a Police Search Officer (POLSA) who may then decide to call in the services of the team. We work very closely with the POLSA officers, participating in strategy discussion and often providing the more significant search resource due to available manpower.

Over the years, we have been involved in many high profile missing from home enquiries and tragically, many of these have resulted in fatalities, some through self-harm and misadventure but also some that have been the result of murder.

Our approach follows a set of theory bases that provide behavioural profiles for a range of missing person types. This includes despondent people, missing toddlers, teenagers and those with memory loss. The TL will, along with the police, draw up a profile of the missing person. This will include interviews with their family and from this, a set of priority search areas will be established, based upon the theories on how they are likely to behave.

The Team will then apply a range of search techniques to these areas, with the aim of increasing the probability of detection to as high a level as possible. Many variables will affect this; day, night and weather being some of them. Terrain will also affect the search technique.

We will use hasty searches, more detailed shoulder-to-shoulder searches and, of course, utilise our search dogs in detecting human scent on the air. We may use noise or light to attract attention to us and will frequently be supported by aircraft. This will be the police helicopter or the RAF, both of which have thermal imaging capability. Often we will search the same ground over and over using different approaches until we are satisfied that the missing person or any clues to their whereabouts have not been overlooked.

This is an extract from an article from the Mountain Rescue Magazine that describes the thinking behind a search for a missing Alzheimer's sufferer. This took place in an urban setting in County Durham and was written by the TL - DBS:

Placing faith in missing person behaviour statistics

It is 22.30 hrs and the mobile rings. No one I know - a private number, this usually means the police. Especially at this time, and I am right. An Alzheimer's sufferer in his mid 80's has been missing since mid-morning in a large conurbation. The POLSA officer has just been alerted, and knowledgeable of the urgency in such scenarios, and time elapsed, immediately consults the Team. Thirty-five minutes later, I am at the police station gathering information.

The missing person lives at the edge of a large town. Place Last Seen (PLS) at home at 11.30hrs. Advanced stages of Alzheimer's and has been missing before, including a very recent wander. He used to live, work and socialise at the far side of the town, some 4 miles distant. Previous wanderings utilised the bus corridor he lived on, which gave direct routes to this other side. A few weeks prior, he was found walking the bus route in the area he used to socialise.

Now, a possible Last Known Place (LKP), a sighting of him at 15.00 hrs, near this same location - some 3.5 miles from home. Surrounding terrain was mixed. Housing, industrial estates, parkland and disused railway corridors leading straight out into open countryside. So where do we start? Police were undertaking road searches and had used air support and dogs to check around where he lived, and now the plan was focusing on clearing random cemeteries and parkland areas throughout the town.

My mind cast back to countless previous Alzheimer's searches and the talk given by Robert Koester at the Bangor MRC Conference. The possible LKP, earlier wandering history to this area, and regression behaviour pointed strongly to the area of town well away from where he lived and as I sat in the police station, the activity and thought processes going on around me added more focus to this developing theory that he had, again, crossed the town and LKP would be the starting point.

It is so easy to go with the flow, especially when your team are gathering in the Police car park, awaiting briefing, and wondering whether they can get some sleep, before work.

You start to develop your own hunches, and the pressure to 'stab in the dark' around the map builds. You resist. Self-talk kicks in - 'get it right' - 'apply the theory'. The POLSA is a welcome ally. My well-thumbed Missing Person Behaviour Stats file opens. The reported LKP, repetitive wandering and regression behaviour point strongly to this area well away from his PLS, his home. This cannot be ignored. But neither can the reported 70% of wandering 'finds' within 1 km of the PLS and natural entrapment of streams, ditches and boundaries.

A small area some 400m from his home is identified. Open grass, a few trees and a small stream. Previously searched by Police dogs and Air support, and subsequently discounted in lieu of possible LKP sighting.

Robert Koester's story at the conference, of simple application of theory to complicated search areas rings true. A plan quickly formulates. The complexities of urban mapping and geography are stripped away, a small-grassed area with stream stands out - this becomes the initial priority, against the flow of opinion on the LKP. Search teams are deployed. Within 40 minutes a body is found in the small stream, only 400m from his home. The missing person inquiry is resolved within 2 hours of the team being called.

The possible LKP, whilst fitting past behaviour and much of the missing person stats, was likely to have been borne from mistaken identity, based upon a genuine desire to find the missing person. It carried with it a degree of genuine logic and expectation that could have diverted search responses well away from where the missing person was. Robert Koester made the point that we must remain guided by known facts and not be mistakenly diverted by the complexities of 'other' evidence and terrain complications.

Alzheimer's behaviour wandering outcomes are to an extent predictable and, as such, any search plan must as an initial priority, mirror this prediction. Thank you Mr Koester and the Missing Person Behaviour statistics - again!

Robert Koester saw the article from his home in the USA and replied:

> *Dear David,*
>
> *Thanks for passing on the article. I too would have been tempted to send a lot of resources across town. But as you so aptly pointed out, that small area nearby would have leaped out at me also. It's also great you have well trained resources that can search well at night. That makes all the difference also. Oh, just a little thing. Alzheimer's should be capitalized and it usually gets the apostrophe thing since the full name is Alzheimer's disease. Once again thanks for sending along the article and thanks for getting me up in the middle of the night to use the data. Very few researchers ever get to see someone actually use their research, the fact that search and rescue planners such as yourself use it, is deeply satisfying. Hope to get back to the UK soon.*
>
> *Bob Koester*

The following is the story of one of the biggest searches in the team's history. Alan Best tells the story.

The search for Harry Gustard

Mr Gustard, 44 years old, was a town councillor and ex-mayor of Seaham. He had left no clues at all in his car when it was found just outside Stanhope the evening after he had been reported missing in early October 1994. Mr Gustard was a regular experienced fell walker in Weardale who usually took his German Shepherd dog with him, but had not on this occasion. He also used to work in the mines.

The initial phase of the search was based upon this very limited information, identifying and searching routes that could have been followed from the car. The Police helicopter, in use for the first time, in such a search was tasked to cover these routes and local gamekeepers were asked to cover their patches. Team members deployed as they arrived from work, Police horses, Dog Des and Police Dog Handlers.

There are many pressures at the start of a search - tasks to be recorded, plans developed for the next phase, but when should this be? When was to be the point of calling in other teams, when did it get dark, when was the optimum time to get teams to Stanhope to have daylight in which to search if the initial response did not find Mr Gustard.

Winching on excercise

The Team Leader was becoming the Search Manager. We were not to know it that morning, but this was to become the largest search, with the greatest commitment of man-hours by Mountain Rescue teams in the North of England since Lockerbie, spanning over three weeks. By late morning, we had searched paths and many of the places that could have caused someone to have a mishap. No evidence at all.

To expand the search to the multitude of disused quarries nearby, we instigated a NESRA callout including the RAF Mountain Rescue team at Leeming. They were first to arrive within an hour of the callout. Their arrival was spectacular, the transit Control vehicle began to shake and its metal panels vibrate in a deafening, deep thudding as a Chinook helicopter hovered overhead landing in the field next to Control. Their Team Leader explained that the crew of the Chinook had stopped off for a break at Leeming on a flight from Oldham in Hampshire to Otterburn when the call had come in so they were offered a lift! They were followed shortly after by a Sea King to help in the search and to deploy teams.

At this stage, we were working on the assumption that Mr Gustard was laid injured somewhere. In the following days, the search became a major incident. Teams from NESRA and Swaledale Team's cave rescuers and other support slept overnight in a hall in Stanhope as the search expanded. We worked hard to plan the searches based upon the Police work undertaken by the then Inspector David Jones with house-to-house inquiries and further interviews with the family.

The family were brought up to Stanhope, for us to ask further questions. Public appeals for information were undertaken, which although felt important by the family, we knew could add confusion and false hope. We had learnt in other searches that posters and television appeals could put the missing person anywhere. In this case, from Ullswater to Leeds to the Highlands and most other walking areas in between. The responses all needed Police Officers' time to sift through and ascertain what information might be relevant.

It was in fact word of mouth amongst local people that revealed a number of clues. A number of people had seen Mr Gustard with his dog in the past often heading South on footpaths up toward Sharnberry, and the Elephant Trees (a small collection of trees that from a distance does uncannily resemble elephants) on the watershed between Weardale and Teesdale.

Then a whole new dimension opened when there was a report that Mr Gustard had been seen on the Sunday afternoon on a path that could lead toward Hamsterley Forest, an area that up to that point had only been searched from the air. Foresters were asked to search tracks and we decided that the area of search was so large we would ask for support from the teams of the East Cumbria Panel (ECP).

For the first time there was a joint search management team from NESRA and East Cumbria co-ordinating a search of over 200 mountain rescuers, cave rescuers, mine exploration groups, a large contingent of Search and Rescue Dogs, Police on horseback, trial bikes and members of the public. The search took place over the following weekend and included the end areas to the North of Stanhope when the priority areas to the south had been cleared.

At the end of such an intense effort over 7 days, if Mr Gustard had been lying injured we should have found him, and we had to begin to think the worst. We had covered an area of over 120 square kilometres.

Over the next two weeks, we turned out on many days to respond to particular reports or sightings. We also tried to systematically search all the mine levels that we could identify. Nothing.

The family understandably would not give up and organised through newspaper appeals several coaches of friends, and asked members of the public to turn up to support the search. Again, we tried to co-ordinate this with Team Members out with each group, to ensure a safe and structured search.

One afternoon I was called at work to say that Mr Gustard's son was above Frosterley and had found where he thought his father had fallen into an airshaft. We called out the crag team and met at a shaft which had already been searched by the Cave Rescuers but, to ensure a further search clarified matters for his distraught son, we rigged up our tripod and a Team Member went down into the gloom but to no avail.

On another evening, Dog Des found a level to the North of Stanhope that was overgrown and not marked on the map, where Spot (the search dog) also 'indicated'. With great anticipation, we entered the level to find a dead sheep.

Another lasting memory for Des, was on the third day of the search, when trying to save time following yet more fresh information, a local shepherd offered to take Des up onto the Fell from where shouting had been heard. Des clambered aboard a quad bike with the shepherd, and set off on the 'urgent response'. A few moments later with Des lying in a ditch, Spot was still running off alongside the farmer. We think Des prefers to walk these days!

After three weekends and countless evenings, Inspector Jones and I met with the family to go though every detail of what we had done and to say that from the Team's point of view we could commit no more time to the search, that we had done all we could. It was a very difficult decision to make but we had followed every relevant lead to find nothing.

Two weeks later, I was helping with a NESRA search management weekend in Cleveland. On the Saturday night, the pager went off with a message to phone Inspector Jones. He described the horror faced by an amateur geologist who was looking for minerals deep in a mine in Blanchland, Northumberland, where he was once a miner. There are 7 miles of tunnel in this particular mine and in one of these, the man turned the corner to find a body hanging from a beam. The body was recovered by colleagues of the Northumberland Team.

Evidence found at the place of the hanging later lead the coroner to decide that Mr Gustard had deliberately taken his own life.

It would appear that on the Sunday Mr Gustard had left his car, and first set out toward Hamsterley and allowed himself to be seen. The mine where he had taken his life was, in a straight line, almost 14km away from his parked car in the opposite direction! Of all the sightings, reports of previous walks or descriptions of exploration of mines through three weeks of the search nothing at all suggested Mr Gustard would have gone in this direction.

One of the reasons that we eventually searched the mines well to the North of Stanhope was that Team Leader, Dave Thompson, had been contacted many years before in another search, by a Medium who said that she had information that she felt could help in the search for a missing man. When the dead person was later found by a member of the public walking his dog, there had been similarities between the place and that described by the medium. We reached a point in the search for Mr Gustard where we had followed up every lead so the Medium was invited up to Stanhope Police Station and given a few key pieces of information about Mr Gustard but nothing about what we had done in the search. A large map of the search area was

Swift water training - Upper River Tees

laid out on a table. The Medium held a pendant over the point where the car had been left. The pendant first began swinging in a circle then backwards and forwards along a line North East to South West above the car. We later realised that the entrance to the mine, which was not on our search map, where Mr Gustards' body was found, lay on this line if it was extended!

Technical Water Rescue – John Little

TWSMRT has always had connections with water. The Team was founded following a life lost in Maize Beck and a wide range of water incidents continue to occupy the Team's time. This isn't surprising given the numerous rivers, including the Tees and the Wear draining County Durham as well as the numerous reservoirs. An additional and increasingly important aspect, which the team is now better prepared for than ever, is rescues and searches during floods.

Members are trained to one of three different levels. All Team Members train in basic water awareness - this training covers the main dangers of the water environment and the most basic of steps to minimise risk. The training also covers basic hydraulics although a detailed understanding is not expected until later.

Following on from awareness training, most Team Members are trained to allow them to operate safely on riverbanks and near water - this, in reality, is where most of our time in water-related incidents is spent. Searching riverbanks is very challenging - they are often steep, overgrown and slippery. Sometimes rope-based access is necessary, but this is in practice too slow to be used to search large areas and other techniques are often employed instead. A particularly useful technique is to scan the river left bank while standing on the river right bank and vice-versa.

Team Members trained to operate on the bankside also have to practice for accidental immersion by swimming in white water and rescuing fellow Team members using Talk, Reach and Throw techniques. In order to do this safely, Team Members also start training to 'read the water' - this allows them to accurately predict where a person in the water is going to end up and hence where to position a rescue.

A small, but increasing number of Team Members are also now trained to operate in the water. Following on from the Awareness and Bankside levels of training, Team Members complete an intensive three days' further training, covering a wide range of additional Bankside and in-water rescue techniques as well as night searching and night swimming.

These Team Members will also commit extra days to additional training - as making sure a water rescue is successful every time takes a great deal of regular practice. The extra training allows more time for practising things like weir rescue that involve putting a team member into what can be a very dangerous environment.

Technical Rope Rescue - Paul Renwick

Technical Rope Rescue or 'Crag Rescue' as it's commonly known, has had its ups and downs over the past forty years!

Should the team use single, double or even three ropes in a rescue? This has always been an issue. We decided that two ropes were the way forward (one working line, one as safety) and the next question arose, should we use dynamic or static rope and should we raise or lower? Once these questions were answered, someone made different colour ropes! Should we use red for safety or for working?

TWSMRT have always maintained the ability to perform rope rescues throughout County Durham with places in their remit such as Cronkley, Holwick Scar and High Force waterfall, which are visited by thousands of people every year. County Durham also has a large number of used and disused quarries that are a huge magnet to children.

Many of these areas have what is known as a 'pre-plan' like Holwick Scar that was re-opened for climbing in 2002, and the beautiful High Force waterfall. The rock type of these two areas are of particular interest as they're known as Whin Sill, which, when wet, becomes extremely slippery. Combine this with one of England's most visited waterfalls and inevitably there will be accidents!

The Team have always trained for such incidents but over a three year period, starting in 2006, the Team took a review of their systems by inviting the MR Head of Training to examine them. There are many different systems out there, all with their own merits – Our original system, Industrial Rope Access Trade (IRATA),

Rigging4Rescue (Canadian), Oldham Rope Rescue course, to name but a few. The Team decided to 'steal' the best practices from all of them to create a new, bespoke rope rescue system for ourselves.

This new system was then re-reviewed by the same bearded man from the MR (sorry Mike) with excellent results. To quote Mike Margeson:

'The Crag Team have quite evidently made a significant and major step forward over the last year with modern and effective rope rescue systems now in place with an excellent training manual of the Team's rope rescue procedures. It was clear that the smaller new Crag Team had a much higher level of skills.'

The Team decided to pass on this new knowledge and training to other Teams. In 2008, it ran the first ever regional Technical Rope Rescue Course, inviting all six NESRA Teams. Many friends have been made throughout this review of rope techniques and without their contribution, the results may not have been so pleasing. Bill Batson was a particular fountain of knowledge.

The Team's skill level has continued to improve and now with a monthly training programme including visits to the Lakes (with Keswick Mountain Rescue Team) and the Cairngorms, they continue to progress and hone their training.

Over the past forty years, the team have responded to a number of incidents, dogs down mine shafts, birds of prey stuck in trees, sheep stuck on quarry faces, people falling off things, including definitely the most peculiar callout I encountered, which was one Sunday morning around 0200hrs.

A report of a man falling off the roof of his house and landing on scaffolding was received. Police, Fire and Ambulance services were in attendance.

The man was being treated for head and spinal injuries and the team were required to assist with the extraction of the man from the scaffolding. Having placed him onto the Team's stretcher, it was decided that, for safety reasons, the male should allow Police to put a pair of handcuffs on him to prevent him falling off. The man refused to allow Police to place the cuffs on, but would allow a Team Member to do so! It was never fully explained why he ended up in that predicament!

Casualty Care - Richard Warne

Think of the last First Aid course you did…what was the underlying theme? As with all good basic first aid it would have involved stabilising the casualty and do no further harm until help arrives. A good theory, until you're almost three thousand feet up a hill on craggy terrain, miles from the nearest road and out of reach of even the most intrepid helicopter crews due to the snowstorm blowing around you. Welcome to the world of the Mountain Rescue Medic!

Pre-hospital medical care has evolved tremendously over the past forty years and Mountain Rescue has had to keep up. From the early days of utilising the nearest five-bar gate as a stretcher and a first aid sack containing ex-army wound dressings and a bar of Kendal mint cake, right up to today's state of the art vacuum mattress, drugs and patient monitors, Mountain Rescue Casualty Care has developed and improved to provide the best possible treatment in the worst possible conditions.

Medical training for all Team Members starts from day one, and it is an expectation that all probationary Team Members have undertaken some form of basic first aid training prior to joining the Team. The reason for this is simple. The very nature of the work we do as a Team is hazardous, and even in training Team Members may often be miles from the nearest road and isolated from any form of assistance, so it is vital that everyone has at least the basic skills to look after their colleagues should an accident befall them.

The next step is to train everyone in Basic Life Support (BLS), which is an extension of the standard CPR techniques taught on most first aid courses. BLS hones the individual's skill at performing CPR and introduces the use of oxygen therapy, airway adjuncts and suction devises so that the rescuer can better manage their patient should they suffer a cardiac or respiratory arrest.

Training in the use of defibrillators is also provided; again, to increase the chances of survival of any casualty we may deal with who suffers a cardiac arrest.

This training is especially useful given the large geographical spread of our Team Members. It has been quite common for our Team Members to happen upon incidents of this nature in their normal daily lives and to put these skills to good effect.

Following on from BLS training comes the core standard that most Team Members attain within their first two years of training. This is known as the Basic Mountain Rescue Casualty Care course. This course follows a national syllabus and is assessed and certified by our governing body, Mountain Rescue (England and Wales). The course itself is anything but basic and requires a significant amount of time, effort and study by all candidates undertaking it. Teaching skills and techniques not dissimilar to those used by road-side ambulance crews, the basic 'cas-care' course goes on to prepare rescuers to stabilise and maintain their patients over extended periods in extreme conditions.

Rescuers are trained in the use of an array of medical equipment from patient monitors and stretchers through to traction splints and vacuum mattresses. Skills such as injection techniques are taught to facilitate the administration of the range of therapeutic drugs available, including strong painkillers such as morphine and lifesaving drugs such as adrenaline. The course culminates in an assessment, which usually takes place regionally over the course of a weekend.

There are four sections to the assessment, which must all be successfully completed in order to gain the qualification. The first is a practically based BLS assessment whereby the candidate must demonstrate competency on a resuscitation manikin in front of a nurse/paramedic.

The next stage is an examination paper that covers all aspects of the course including medication doses and effects.

The final two stages of the assessment are conducted by doctors and require candidates to deal with actors wearing full casualty make-up known as moulages. Competency in both trauma and medical situations must be shown in order to pass.

Once all this has been completed, successful candidates usually head straight for the nearest pub to drink away the stress, congratulate themselves and look forward to doing it all again in three years time!

My first experience of casualty care came when I joined the Team as a Cadet (now known as the Youth Team) at the age of seventeen. I had never really been into first aid and to be honest, as a small child I was usually frightened by the St Johns Ambulance first aiders who seemed to patrol around the summer fayres and firework displays in packs, carrying conspicuous looking bum bags!

My first experience of cas-care within the team however was about to change my outlook forever. During one training session, we were introduced to an 'Advanced Medic' by the name of Neil. Neil had undergone a significant amount of further training and his 'broad ranging' sense of humour was an instant hit with our group. He talked us through some of the equipment the Team carried, some basic hints and tips and told us stories of gruesome incidents the Team had dealt with over the years.

For some unknown and slightly sick reason these tales had us baying for the sight of blood and so Neil kindly obliged us by volunteering our Cadet Leader David (now the Team Leader!) to have a great big needle shoved in the back of his hand!

Whether David would have willingly volunteered himself without the pressure of his Cadet group eagerly staring at him remains to be seen, but what followed has stayed with me ever since and kick started my passion for all things medical.

As David nervously sat himself down, Neil prepared his equipment, pulling out what had to be the largest needle I had ever seen in my life, holding it in the air so that the sun glinted off the razor sharp tip. At this point, David's recently acquired tan seemed to drain away to a pasty white and we all nervously giggled with excitement as the needle moved ever closer to his hand.

As Neil proceeded with the cannulation, the words 'sharp scratch' were immediately followed by 'bloody hell Dave, you've got skin tougher than a pig's backside!' A loud 'pop' was heard, followed by a quantity of David's blood flowing down his hand and dripping off his fingers. That was it - I was hooked!

Youth Team with their Icelandic counterparts on Scafell Pike

A year later saw me moving from the Cadets and training as a probationary member of the Team. I got myself on the first available Basic Casualty Care course and read every book on the subject I could get hold of. I wanted to be a medic too!

The Advanced Casualty Care course is developed and administered by the NESRA medical sub-committee. It builds on the knowledge and skills base of the basic course, moving it up a couple of levels to give the advanced medic the ability to better assess their casualty, provide a higher level of treatment and co-ordinate the medical response to large scale incidents.

Mountain Rescue Advanced Medics are trained in many of the skills familiar to ambulance paramedics and are able to deliver a wider range of drugs, intravenous fluids and potentially life saving techniques to better care for the casualty. Advanced medics also take part in the training of rescuers at a basic level.

Access to the advanced course is long and arduous. Prospective candidates must normally have been a member of a rescue team for at least two years and completed at least two basic courses with a high pass mark. A number of assessment weekends follow to determine whether the candidate has the confidence and competence to undertake advanced training. The advanced course instructors are all paramedics or doctors with extensive knowledge of pre-hospital care. Guest lecturers come from around the region and beyond in the form of accident and emergency consultants, consultant cardiologists and orthopaedic surgeons to name but a few. Training is also delivered in psychiatric illness and psychological trauma.

Culmination of the advanced course is again examination and assessment by doctors, with certification lasting two years. Once certified, advanced medics must undertake Continuous Professional Development, by spending time with ambulance service road crews, rapid response units and in accident and emergency departments.

I completed my first advanced course in the Easter of 2004 and loved every minute of it. Despite the array of new skills and techniques we had all been taught, and all the impressive sounding drugs we could now administer, one thing had become apparent - that it is the basics done well, that saves lives. As I left the course sporting my shiny new 'star of life' badge and bursting with confidence, all I wanted was for a chance to put my newfound knowledge to the test. I was to get it a little over a week after getting home from the course.

Saturday afternoon my pager went off. It read 'IMMEDIATE CALL OUT. INJURED PERSON IN MINE COLLAPSE 600FT UNDERGROUND.' As the Team arrived on scene, we could see that the fire and rescue services were already there as was the ambulance service. An American mineral prospector had been collecting samples with friends down an old disused drift mine when there had been a partial roof collapse, trapping him under tonnes of debris.

Fire fighters had managed to free the man and bring him to the tunnel entrance where paramedic crew began assessing him for injuries. The only problem was that the tunnel entrance emerged 60ft up a sheer cliff face and the light was fading. This is where we came in. As the team got to work setting up rope systems to lower the casualty down to the ground, an RAF Search & Rescue helicopter was scrambled from 202 Squadron RAF Boulmer.

The casualty was placed into one of our vacuum mattresses (A full body splint that forms around the casualty then goes rigid, supporting injuries, preventing further damage through handling and providing insulation) and then strapped into one of our stretchers in preparation for the lift. I took over medical care of the patient from the ambulance crew.

The middle aged man had sustained bi-lateral fractures to his femurs (thigh bones), a fractured pelvis, suspected spinal trauma, broken ribs, was hypothermic and was developing a pneumothorax (where damage to the lung causes air to leak into the chest cavity and causes the lung to collapse).

This was the sort of thing I had been dreaming about doing ever since that first day as a Cadet but I wasn't smiling.

This gentleman was seriously ill and had very little going for him. I was desperate not to lose my first patient as an advanced medic.

Thankfully, the helicopter arrived quickly and I was soon being winched up 200ft into the big noisy yellow 'bird' overhead. The casualty and winch man followed and the pilot wasted no time in setting course for the hospital.

Meanwhile, back at home, Team Medics began treating the remaining members of the mining party who by now were in a state of emotional shock, hypothermia and exhaustion. A couple of them had sustained minor head injuries when the roof had collapsed and so were transported to hospital by both County and the rescue Team ambulances.

Once I arrived at the hospital, the trauma team took over and began trying to piece back together the damage. As they worked, it became apparent just how extensive the injuries were but the good news was, that they were confident he would 'make it.'

A short while later, the ambulances from the incident arrived and I was reunited with other Team Medics who had been there. As we collected our equipment and headed off back to Base we talked of our relief at a job well done and commented on how well all the emergency services had worked together in bringing the incident to a successful conclusion.

After a stay in hospital, the injured gentleman recovered and is now back to collecting minerals from disused mines again. As for us, we all took something away from that incident, mine in particular being, be careful what you wish for - it might just come true!

At the time of writing, the Team has a significant proportion of its Members qualified to basic level, a number waiting for the next course and the highest level of Advanced Medics in the Team's history. A number of Team Members have also undertaken training with the North East Ambulance Service to become Community First Responders, delivering emergency care to high-risk patients across the county.

The level of pre-hospital emergency care provided by the Team continues to grow, with its Members giving their time (and blood, sweat and tears) freely and receiving no payment for their services or dedication. Medical equipment and disposables cost a vast amount of money, so spare a thought next time you venture out into the hills and don't be surprised if you see Rescue Team Medics at Street collections raising money to buy the latest equipment for use on their next 'victim'!

Youth Section - Chris Roberts

TWSMRT are unique in having the only known Youth Team Section in the UK. A number of full members on the Team today have progressed from the Youth Team where it is open to young people between the ages of 16 and 18 years old with an interest in outdoor activity and the work carried out by search and rescue teams.

The group meet once a month, usually on the Sunday prior to, or after, the Team's weekend training exercise. Training involves all aspects of mountain craft, both out on the hill, and indoors at the Base. The programme roughly follows the modules of MLTB (Mountain Leadership Training Board) with some of the Youth Section participating in various award schemes themselves such as the Duke of Edinburgh Awards. It is a fantastic way of gaining experience, which also offers many exciting opportunities.

Youth Section - You're not from 'round here!!!

Chris Roberts, Deputy Team Leader, was involved in the Youth Section for many years and here he talks about the Youth Team's expeditions.

In 2002, the Team put together a very ambitious funding bid with North Pennines LEADER+. The bid was to support many areas of development for the Team including vehicles, training, equipment and development of our Youth Section.

Something else caught my eye on the application form - funding for Trans national projects - Why not give it a go?

The main bid with the North Pennines LEADER+ was successful. We got the news early in 2003, and it was of major benefit to the Team and allowed us to take forward many projects that had otherwise seemed out of reach.

What of the Trans National Project? It seemed like the ideal opportunity to take on with the Youth Section, but where? The project needed to be within Europe as the funding was European money. Our Deputy at the time, now Team Leader, had spent some time in Iceland and knew that the Icelandic Team now embraced the idea of involving young people in their search and rescue teams, of which there are many.

The idea was floated with the funders, who seemed enthusiastic. It would need to be a separate bid so more forms needed to be filled in.

All went quiet, and to be honest, I had forgotten about the project until I got a phone call out of the blue in September 2003 - the project had been approved, when were we planning on going? A period of frantic e-mailing ensued as I contacted ICESAR (Icelandic Search and Rescue) for contacts. I was put in touch with their Youth Development Officer and plans were made.

Six weeks later myself, my assistant leader, and one of our current Youth Section set off to Iceland. We had an amazing week visiting Bases around the Reykjavik area, meeting like-minded people. Icelandic rescue teams see their youth as the lifeblood of teams in the future - a pity we don't do more of that here in the UK!

The week had filled us with enthusiasm and the idea of an exchange visit between our Youth Section and one of the Icelandic teams seemed like a great idea and of potential benefit to our Team and hopefully set a path for other teams in the UK.

There followed a period of planning and negotiation with several teams in Iceland. A funding application was submitted for an exchange to take place over the summer of 2005. In early 2005 - we had a partner team to exchange with, dates had been set and everything looked fine - as they say in every good film; 'It's quiet, too quiet'. Spot on - a bombshell!

Some of our group were apparently not eligible to receive funding as they lived outside the area. How did we anticipate funding them came the question?

Simple, we can't!

In that moment, everything collapsed. I rang people up, sent grumpy e-mails, but in the end had to cancel the plans. We went to the Cairngorms instead.

What a great week we had. Wild camping at 1500m, rain, fog, a bit of snow and some brilliant sunshine - a typical Scottish summer. But it wasn't the Icelandic trip I had been planning for so long!!

Youth Section - The Visit 2006

Later on that year came another shot out of the blue. The funders could see the merit in our exchange and wanted to find a way round the funding issues. Several meetings later and we were back in the game.

Did we still have an exchange partner?

I contacted the leader at the team we had planned to stay with. Their Base had burned down during the lead up to Christmas and New Year - Icelandic Rescue teams sell all the fireworks for the New Year celebrations - ironically this particular team's stocks had caught fire, destroying the Base; and the leader was also now on his way back to the States to start a new career.

Back to frantic e-mailing - the Youth Leader had moved on after having a baby, so that contact was out of the picture. I got in touch with a guy in ICESAR who I had met at the MRC conference. After a short time, he got back to me with several teams wanting to exchange, in particular the team from Isafjordur in the NW of the country. Hastily we got together and made a plan.

That year, summer 2006, they would visit us and the following year we would go to them - easy. And it was- relatively. Summer 2006, 10 young people from Iceland plus their leaders came over here. We showed them around Teesdale - they loved the trees (not too many in Iceland). An Icelandic joke. What do you do if you get lost in Iceland? Stand up!

The biggest waterfall in England (High Force) didn't impress them quite as much however!

Icelandic teams often have a lifeboat attached to them so visits to Hartlepool and Sunderland lifeboat stations were well received - the Isafjordur team's boat at the time had been purchased from Tynemouth.

The Lake District made a big impression - we spent several days walking taking in Scarfell and Helvellyn.

The ten days flew by and we parted good friends, already looking forward to our return in 2007. In the lead up to our visit, the group needed to get together some extra funds for team kit - we particularly wanted polo shirts and fleeces that gave us a team identity. 'Bag packing' at the local supermarket always gets a good response, so a big thanks to the generous shoppers at Morrisons in Barnard Castle.

More impressive was the sponsored Everest climb on the team training wall; the Youth Team climbed non-stop until the equivalent of Everest had been climbed - a brilliant effort (yet another example the young people are worth it!!).

Youth Section - Iceland Trip 2007

July 2007 and we are on a plane to Iceland - hard to believe after all the pit falls along the way.

The ten day visit started with the group being taken on the 'Golden Circuit' – the main tourist attractions around the Reykjavik area, which takes in the spectacular Gulfoss waterfall, the geysers in the Geysir region and the site of the ancient parliament at Thingvellir.

To relax after the tour, the group then bathed in the luxury of the Blue Lagoon – the geothermal pools on the outskirts of Reykjavik.

The first experience of an Icelandic Search and Rescue Team for the Youth Team was at Grindavik, a small town on the coast to the South West of Reykjavik. The Team here has a fine history of land and sea rescues.

Unlike teams in the UK where the standard vehicle is a Land Rover, here the garage housed a top specification Land Cruiser and an ex NATO Forward Command Vehicle. The young people were treated to a ride along the rugged larval coast in this monster - going 'off road' like no other vehicle they had experienced!

Less exciting, but never the less very interesting was a visit to the Coastguard HQ where the group was given a tour of the Base and given an understanding of the role of coastguard helicopters in Iceland. There was also a visit to Iceland's oldest rescue team base – a Team which boasts two recent Everest climbers.

ICESAR Headquarters was next. This is a facility shared by all the emergency services. In a basement there is a command centre designed for managing major incidents.

The next three days were spent at Gufuskalar - the ICESAR training centre positioned at the remote eastern end of the Snaefellsnes peninsula. This facility is special because it has one of the few earthquake training areas in the West.

The Youth Team were given an introduction to the site and a tour of the tunnels and collapsed building. They were then given a search and rescue scenario and had to organise and carry out a casualty search and recovery. They were pretty impressive, particularly when they emerged from one of the tunnels hauling a stretcher, together with casualty.

With our guide, Thor, an afternoon was spent exploring some of the caves formed from volcanic activity. For one of these, together with the Icelandic youth members, a crevasse rescue system was set up and members of the group were lowered individually into a deep cave.

This cave had last been explored in the early 90's as evidenced by a message left by the cavers. Particularly interesting were the skeletal remains of a family of arctic foxes that had somehow found their way into, but not out of, the cave.

I was very impressed by the slickness of the setting up of the rescue rigging. I asked the Icelanders how often they practised using this piece of kit – "First time", was the reply – of course; silly me!

The training centre and indeed the whole peninsular is dominated by the conically shaped, now dormant volcano Snaefellsjokull at 1446m. In Jules Vernes's story 'Journey to the Centre of the Earth,' the explorers begin their journey here, emerging sometime later at Stromboli volcano in Italy!

Our next day was spent climbing Snaefellsjokull. For some members of the group this was their first experience of 'winter' climbing. Once at the top, great views could be enjoyed – some continued to the summit proper gaining experience in the use of ice axe and crampons.

Getting to the host Team's town of Isafjordur, took a full day of driving and a 4 hour ferry crossing. Whilst the scenery was outstanding – passing waterfalls with minor drops that dwarf our High Force.

Described by one of our hosts as, 'The never ending journey,' it can be very frustrating travelling along the Icelandic roads and tracks, as they tend to follow the coastline rather than going more direct.

Isafjordur is the largest settlement in the Northwest fjords area, having around 3,500 inhabitants. It has a long history as a trading port and today has in important fishing industry; it also acts as the commercial and cultural centre of the area.

The team here operates, as many others in the country, both land and sea rescues.

The first day was spent trying out the team's Zodiacs (fast inshore rescue boats); some of the time inside the boat, but an equal amount of time, in the water. It was particularly good fun being towed at high speed hanging on to an inflated tyre!

For all of these 'wet' activities, the Youth Team members were dressed in survival immersion suits – as many will testify these were not quite as waterproof as one might have hoped - all being second hand! It did of course provide a photo opportunity for the local newspaper.

At the time the Isafjordur Team used a lifeboat previously based at Tynemouth (they have since bought a newer boat from the RNLI). It was this boat that was to take us on our two day mini expedition.

The trip started with whale watching in the fjord – we were lucky enough to see a pair of Minky whales, which was a great high for everyone. After about two hours sailing we were dropped off at the now mainly uninhabited settlement of Grunnavik.

From there we walked for about three hours to our camp site at Flaedaryri, once the home area of one of our host's grandparents. This was a beautiful place looking towards a glacier at the end of the fjord. There was a summer house owned by the relatives of the original inhabitants of the area, which we used to make the coffee that was essential to keep me going!

We got an insight into the Icelandic psyche (or at least that of the young generation) whilst there. I asked one of our hosts what time we were going to settle down. The answer was basically, if I was tired, I should go to bed, if not then stay up; the same applied to getting up in the morning. It should be remembered that we were there during the summer and it never really got dark.

All that being said we did have a deadline to meet as the lifeboat came to pick us up - around midday.

Our last day in Iceland was spent on the long drive back to Reykjavik – a last chance to take in the awe-inspiring scenery that is Iceland. We had a couple of hours to explore the city of Reykjavik followed by a celebration dinner in one of the city's oldest buildings, which by chance does a very good meal!

The purpose of the exchange was to give the group the opportunity to learn about rescue techniques used by other teams, but more than that, it gave a unique insight into how young people can work together with a common aim – working in search and rescue.

In Iceland, it is common for young people to belong to search and rescue teams. In fact, of the 90 odd teams, nearly half encourage the involvement of young people from the age of 14.

It is a wonderful place to visit and terrific hosts made our visit really worthwhile and very enjoyable. I can't wait to go again and see more of this most unique of places

Was it worth it? Ask the group that went - they wouldn't have missed it for the world. What now? I have handed the Youth Team over to a new leader for more adventures. Watch this space.

Canoe Team and History - Tony Hammock

County Durham is patterned with deep river gorges. They contain some of the most beautiful rivers in England, where, over thousands of years, the water has cut through sedimentary layers to find the hardened planes of the Whin Sill. The rivers are fast flowing and, as kayakers would have it, 'interesting'. The flanks of the gorges are often rocky and usually in a tangle of woodland and undergrowth. To carry out a detailed search of the river banks can be extremely difficult, time consuming and a dangerous task.

The stimulus for the creation of the Canoe Team was a sad event in the Woodencroft gorge. A despondent person had found his end there and because of the difficulties already explained, it was some time before his remains were discovered close to the river. Len Smith, a retired fireman and a kayak slalom coach, offered to set up and train a canoe search team. The original team consisted of Len, his son Russ (an ex-world champion slalomist), Tony Hammock and Leo Crosling amongst others. The early exercises were a bit experimental with several lessons learned, some of them rather embarrassing.

On the first search exercise, a number of 'personal effects' were thrown off High Force and a dummy was secreted on the bank lower down the river. The Canoe Team started their search from the pool below the falls, very aware that they were going to have to establish their credibility.

They quickly found some very small items, including a single brown glove, and basked in the praise that flowed from the co-ordinator over the improvised waterproof communications.

The Canoe Team enjoyed a descent of Low Force and reported that they had completed their search sector.

Egos deflated rapidly when the controller, in a voice heavy with exasperation, suggested they should walk back upstream. Crestfallen, the team found the full size (if headless) dummy in full view on the bank above Low Force. Being able to paddle was not enough. A systematic search method was needed.

The first rescue practises were sometimes a bit fraught. The 'proper' Team liked to use ropes and the Canoe Team didn't. Eventually the climbers came to appreciate the dangers of ropes in water and the benefit of floating rope. The kayakers learned that their method of liberating a scared paddler from a mid-river rock - click on a throw line and push him in - was not acceptable in an MR context!

Russ Smith ran an excellent moving water training course for A List Team Members on the White Water course. Lots of people found out that you only need 9 inches of fast flowing water to take your feet out from under you and that sliding down the course on your backside can be rather good fun in controlled conditions.

Some time around 1998 (can't remember exactly when) Len and Russ moved to Stockton to manage the Tees barrage white water course and Tony Hammock took over training and co-ordination of the Team. Several new Members were inducted into the Team including Chris Roberts and Graeme Cranston. Tony, in a fit of enthusiasm, decided that the Team should practice extracting a kayak from a pinned situation.

They took an unwanted plastic kayak to the salmon leap falls between Low and High Force and threw it in above the tight section. It sailed straight through! They tried again and again. It was quite a blow to the paddlers egos to find that a kayak could get down this section without the need of a kayakers skill to guide it.

The reality of the Canoe Teams callouts turned out to be very unglamorous. They came only a couple of times a year, always on a slow, smelly stretch of river and usually on a day earmarked for Christmas shopping.

One search of the River Wear above Durham, however, was enlivened by two events. Firstly, Tony Hammock rounded a bend and, in the midst of his studied concentration, was confronted by a flesh coloured rubber glove floating with air in the fingers. The bow wave of the kayak caused the glove to slowly bob up and down. The resultant shriek could be heard for some distance. Later on, the Police assisted, by picking up the Canoe Team in the centre of Durham using their big riot van to carry the kayaks. At least two paddlers were mortified to hear onlookers speculating on exactly why the kayakers were being arrested.

In time, the Canoe Team demonstrated an ability to find things in a difficult environment that other search methods could not locate. In particular, on two separate occasions, the Canoe Team has located deceased people after multiple unsuccessful searches by walkers, helicopters and police dogs. The Canoe Team earned the appreciation and praise of the police and have become a valued TWSMRT resource.

Police, Mountain Rescue Teams, RAF and the Fire Brigade
– David Bartles-Smith

How these work together/development of links

The Police have responsibility for inland Search and Rescue (SAR) and over past decades, particularly in the main upland areas of the UK, the role of civilian Mountain Rescue Teams has become more and more a feature of the response to a person or persons reported injured or missing.

TWSMRT are fully 'Airwave' enabled which means we carry police radios and can talk direct to the Police and the police helicopter. Shortly, the same will be true of the Fire and Ambulance services. We also have VHF radios and can therefore talk directly to the RAF.

Any SAR incident that requires Mountain Rescue will be activated by the police. The level of autonomy in terms of command will be dependent upon the incident. A missing hill walker will find the Team assuming command and liaising with the Police in terms of what we are progressing on their behalf. A non-hill search, in other words a person missing from home, will have a POLSA involved and greater direction and involvement of the Police, as there will be a range of enquiries ongoing and other actions that the police can do alongside our search role.

We can call upon the assistance of the RAF SAR helicopters and they will provide an aerial search and also rescue and recovery. This can be done by winch if necessary. These helicopters can also be used to move our search groups around and are able to operate at night and in often-marginal weather conditions. We also use the police helicopters and can request the Air Ambulance directly.

Sometimes, when the incident is a rescue, such as from a river gorge or quarry, we will work with the Fire Service. We have a dedicated technical rescue element to the Team and they work alongside the fire crews.

We can find ourselves working alongside a range of other resources that can include Police dogs, Police search teams, Forensics, underwater search teams and some more specialist police resources such as Caderver dogs that seek out human remains.

TWSMRT is part of the North East Search and Mountain Rescue Association (NESRA) and the East Cumbria Panel (ECP). This means we train and associate with large numbers of adjoining MR teams in Yorkshire, Cleveland, Northumberland and Cumbria. In a major search, these resources are often called upon and we can find ourselves anywhere in the North East and Cumbria assisting in large-scale searches.

In recent years, we have found ourselves more involved in networking and partnership work. The TL attends regular POLSA meetings and we have a dedicated Police Liaison Officer. The Team is also represented in a range of groups set up under the auspices of the Civil Contingencies Act and we are written into the County's Emergency Plans. This is very much a growing part of our work and involvement and underlines the role our voluntary service now plays in support of and alongside the full time emergency services.

'Dog Des' with Meg

SARDA

(Search and Rescue Dog Association)

*'I want that dog to find my son on the mountains. That's the standard
I look for. If it's not up to it, you're wasting your time.'*
- Des Toward - SARDA Rep TWSMRT

TWSMRT has, over its' history developed strong working relationships with many other rescue organisations ranging from RAF Mountain Rescue to the Ambulance Service, the Police, and Fire and Rescue and their support collectively is one element that helps bring together the success of the Team and indeed other MR teams nationally.

However, one particular organisation that plays a more prominent role and offers an invaluable resource is the Search and Rescue Dog Association (SARDA). It has only been in recent years that SARDA has become a recognised name amongst the general public despite its formation in 1965. Previously, when thinking about working dogs, their initial thoughts would naturally turn to guide dogs, sheep dogs and police dogs.

SARDA dogs differ somewhat to those mentioned, as they are trained to react to human air scent as opposed to tracking an individuals' scent along the ground.

Their original and primary role is to work in rural areas in high moorland, lowlands and mountain regions searching for lost walkers and climbers. However, in recent years, it has become increasingly common for them to be employed in more of an urban setting, working alongside Police in a range of incidents including searching for missing children and possible victims of crime. In these cases, it is very demanding work, with the dog handlers having to rely heavily on their own skills and resources. If a handler can work on a mountainside or in a forest competently, they just adjust their training and search techniques for urban areas.

In the same time period, one dog can cover the same area as twenty men searching, which really puts into perspective the importance of dogs in search and rescue. The dog's ability to use their sense of smell and detect human scent is effective whether it is working during the day or at night, in good conditions or poor visibility.

Everyone has a scent, no matter how many times you shower! Humans have an identifiable smell which the dog will scent and pick up on.

Human scent is carried through the air and the distance it is carried depends very much on the weather. If there is no wind or it is stormy then the scent will not be carried as far, resulting in the need for shorter sweeps of a search area to compensate.

Once the dog has detected the scent, it will then follow it to the source - hopefully the missing person. The dog is trained to return to the handler, and bark to indicate a 'find' then lead the handler to where the person is.

These dogs are very hard workers and have been known to search in excess of 11 hours, which is impressive.

Brief History of Rescue Dogs

The use of air scenting search dogs is not a new concept. The first formal use in the UK was during the Second World War when dogs were sent out to locate the victims of the London Blitz resulting in saving the lives of many.

Previously, the Red Cross had used dogs successfully during the First World War on battlefields in a bid to save the lives of injured soldiers.

However, the first ever dogs known to be used in Mountain Rescue were St Bernards in Switzerland in the 17th Century. Bernard of Menthon built a Monastery and Inn on the summit of the Great St Bernard Pass in 980 A.D. These buildings served as a refuge and rescue unit for travellers across the pass for many years and the monks frequently found themselves called upon to assist travellers who were lost or avalanched.

St Bernard dogs were originally brought to the hospice as guard dogs and, over time, they began to accompany the monks on their rescue missions. They proved invaluable as guides in horrendous weather conditions and soon they naturally progressed to locating missing persons, and clearly indicating to the monks their whereabouts. Although they may have been the forerunners of the search dogs we see today they were not however, an influential factor in the formation of SARDA.

In 1963, the Leader of Glencoe Mountain Rescue Team, Hamish Maccinnes, realised the importance of search dogs and had the idea of introducing them to the UK. Hamish found that the Swiss Alpine Club had reviewed their avalanche search methods following the Second World War. They had a system which involved 'probing' whereby personnel would insert a rod into the snow to feel about for a body. This method proved slow and although it was effective in retrieving bodies, the chances of finding a victim alive were slim.

Taking into account previous successes involving search dogs, the Swiss Alpine Club decided to train dogs specifically for avalanche rescues. Centres for Avalanche dog training became widespread throughout the Alps and the Red Cross International invited Hamish Maccinnes to one of those centres back in the sixties. He found the visit inspirational and it served to reinforce the idea that indeed there was a valuable role for search dogs in this country.

Today, SARDA is a registered charitable organisation and has enjoyed continued success for over forty years, saving innumerable lives and can now boast over 90 committed, voluntary, handlers and dogs in England alone.

Wales, Scotland, Ireland and England are all member associations, represented by the umbrella organisation NSARDA (National Search and Rescue Dog Association), and therefore, not unlike Mountain Rescue teams, independently rely heavily on donations from the public.

Handlers, Dogs and Training

'Whilst we are out training with dogs, our families are the ones that suffer. Without their support, these dogs would not be available to search for missing people. We also owe a great deal of thanks to the people known as 'bodies' who come out and lie hidden on a wet moor for hours on end in order for our dogs to find them during training exercises, it can't be much fun but they keep coming back for more.'

- Paul Fell, dog handler

TWSMRT have a number of search dogs either fully trained or in training at any given time. The dogs and their handlers are all part of SARDA but before anyone can train their dog, handlers must have been on the 'A' List of a recognised MR Team for a minimum of one year. The reason for this is that SARDA only help train your dog, but the handler will already need to have the necessary MR skills.

A letter of support from the Team is also required before training can commence. SARDA sets very high standards for its' dogs and handlers to reach before allowing them to search alongside Mountain Rescue Teams, including a long and very tough training and assessment programme.

In December 2005, there were only four graded search dogs available from Mountain Rescue Teams to cover the North East, from the Scottish Border to Yorkshire. Due to the efforts of the Teesdale and Weardale Teams dog handlers; in 2009 the Team had 4 graded dogs and a further 3 in training.

Training search and rescue dogs is a long, intensive process, which means handlers must be fully committed and fully prepared to give up a lot of their own time.

The entire training programme can take 18 to 24 months or longer to complete successfully and will start whilst the dogs are still puppies. Like most dogs, pets or otherwise, they need to be socialised with people and other dogs before continuing onto the next stage which is obedience and stock familiarisation.

Stock familiarisation is teaching your dog to ignore sheep, cows and other livestock you would normally find in the countryside. The reason for this is obvious really. Picture the scene - some poor walker is lying somewhere with a broken ankle, alone, desperate to be found and all the while the dog employed to come looking for them takes a fancy to the lovely flock of sheep that is grazing in a nearby field.

In some cases, it could be a life or death situation.

The dog is going to lose all interest in the task in hand if it is tempted to chase sheep and unless the dog is obedient, the handler will find it difficult to rein it back. It is very important the dog does not have interest in these things.

It certainly is not an easy task to train the dogs in this area, especially if they come from farming stock where it is slightly more difficult to get the instincts of herding out of them. Once those seemingly simple steps are completed, the dog will undergo a stock test to ensure it shows no interest in playing 'chase' with livestock.

Two senior dog handlers with farmers and shepherds present, do the stock test in a controlled way, usually at a local farm. The dogs are put into a pen with the sheep to see how they react.

Providing the dogs pass this stage, they will then continue onto the next three steps of the process. The dogs will begin with 1 minute searches looking for a toy that the handler and dog has spent time playing with, then they progress to simple runaways.

This entails the handler remaining with the dog while someone runs and hides behind something, be it a rock, tree or a bush. The dog and handler then go and find them and once the dog gets the idea it is then left to them to go and 'hunt' for them by themselves. This is a great way of involving family members in the training process, especially children.

At the next stage, 'Dogsbodies' come into play. They are positioned in a location always known to the handler and the dogs will work small areas to begin with to find the supposed victims. Dogsbodies will hide in places with varying terrain that tests the dog's durability. The specific hiding places could include up a tree or near water to ascertain whether the dog can sense or smell the scent.

Once the handler has learnt to search with their dog, later in the process, the next task is to search for Dogsbodies without the handler knowing their location.

Once they have become competent and graduated to three-hour searches, both dog and handler are ready for assessment. The assessments will invariably be carried out over a two-day period in the Lake District or Wales where they are tasked with six searches each lasting up to an hour and a half. It is a very difficult and stressful time for the handlers and once the dog is graded, periodic reassessments are necessary throughout their working life to ensure they are up to scratch.

Des Toward is one of the Team's longest standing Members and has been a member of SARDA and TWSMRT for many years. He began life with the Youth Team at the young age of 16 and to his own admission spent his first ten years carrying stretchers until he decided to train his first search dog, Spot.

Spot was a Border Collie/Spaniel Cross who took Des 18 months from beginning training to getting him onto the callout list. Spot had a successful career and worked until his retirement at the age of 12, having had three finds, which sadly included two dead bodies.

When Spot was 9 years old, Des decided to get another dog and work them both together. Meg, a Border Collie, took only 9 months to train and she proved to be one of the best search dogs there was. Amazingly, during one heavy spell of callouts Meg had six finds in 4 months resulting in her being whisked down to London to receive an award from a dog's charity for her amazing work and also received a commendation from the Chief Constable.

One particular incident, which set her apart from some of the other dogs, was a find which most Team Members found astonishing. A guy had gone missing and his parting words to his wife, were that she would never see him again and off he went. His last known location was on a footpath heading towards the river. Des and Meg searched the riverbank half a mile up stream from where the footpath met the river. As they walked past this junction the dog started to act 'funny' and a little further downstream she went to the riverbank and just started to bark and bark and bark. Every time Des tried to take her away, she kept going back to the same spot again and again, barking and barking. The next day, the Team made the decision to investigate the area of water which Meg had indicated to. Two members of the Swaledale MRT went in with wetsuits and sure enough, there was the guys' body hanging onto a mountain bike 15ft underwater. Incredible!

On a further occasion, the Team had a callout to search for another guy, similar story to the last. He had a domestic dispute with his wife and told her she wouldn't see him again. The mans' van was found at some woods by local police and they had started searching with their dogs. They found nothing.

Des and Meg, with Stan White and Paul Fell navigating then were asked to search the area. Meg went bounding on ahead, whilst the others were getting ready, but by the time the boots were on, Meg was running back barking, indicating a find. The guy was found safe and well. A successful conclusion on this occasion.

Time and again, these stories prove the worth of these dogs and their invaluable role as searchers, and they are a credit to the handlers whose commitment and hard work over such a lengthy period, has made it possible for these dogs to work at their best.

Not everyone on the Team is a dog lover, however, all know how beneficial they are as a Team resource and the dogs are held in high regard, as are their handlers.

Here is one final story from Des that just goes to prove how sensitive these dogs' noses are!

During SARDA training at Robin Hood's Bay, a search area was set up around the cliffs. The handlers knew the area that the body was to be placed and set their dogs off on the search. The dogs set off one at a time but bizarrely each one was running off at an angle away from the 'body'.

The dogs were barking and indicating to their handlers to one particular spot but each handler kept on walking, knowing that the location of the body was in a different location.

This happened three or four times. 'What's going on here?' Des thought to himself so he set off with his dog. Sure enough, his dog did the same, ran off to the same spot as the others, indicated to Des and led him in.

Imagine Des' surprise when greeted by an elderly couple leisurely engaged in some afternoon sexual activity! The elderly man turned round on his elbows mid-strike and asked quite perturbed. 'How many more proverbial dogs are coming up here?' 'Oops, sorry Sir'.

Rescuing a dog from down a mineshaft

Stories, Tips and Tricks

David Bartles-Smith
A Good Day Out?

Many years ago, we joined a regional exercise on the North Yorkshire coast - all were there - RAF, several MR teams, Police, RNLI etc. The day started well then went rapidly downhill!

First came the radio message 'We have rolled the Land Rover over' then a pause - then the words 'over'. Initial silence and incredulity at the double 'over' was soon responded to by assistance to that team - fortunately with no serious injury incurred.

Shortly after that, it was my turn as navigator in our Land Rover to misdirect the driver onto a Special Rally stage - a fact we only became aware of when a disgruntled looking crash helmeted pair in a Subaru Impreza loomed up behind us very quickly and then left us in a cloud of dust and verbals!

Not to be outdone, an hour or so later, the RNLI, in front of us all, decided to dump their inshore boat on to the shingle beach from the crest of a swell - with the outboard engines down!! Oh dear. The RAF decided then it was better to go home, just in case.

 Top Tip **Cut out a piece of plastic bag the size of your boot sole - put it in between your boot and crampon - stops the snow balling up. Can look a mess though. DBS**

Smelly kit!

For weeks, Stan had complained of the atrocious smell emanating from the rear of the Land Rover. Finally after one very wet training exercise, Neil took matters into his own hands and pulled the equipment out. Nothing unusual to be found, but the emergency hill rucksack, unopened in years, seemed to be the culprit. It was duly opened and hidden inside the rolled up sleeping bag, was a present – presumably from a past Team Member, now re-constituted - we never got to the bottom of this one.

Dealing with the job

The finding of and recovery of a body is dealt with respect and dignity. Often some of us in the Team have already met with the person's relatives as part of our search planning and frequently families will send a note of appreciation at a later date. Sometimes the circumstances of the find make it more poignant than others and at times the Team has to extend its' usual support to Team Members in these circumstances.

Team members will deal with the immediate scenario by supporting each other, often by diversionary banter. There are many memorable exchanges and current and past team members will read this, understand and no doubt recall such moments.

Avoid overheating by using the side vents on the jacket.
Paul Allison

Chris Roberts
Lunch – the most important meal of the day?

One of my first callouts with the Team, was searching for a gentleman missing from home. The search area was woodland surrounding a housing estate. The ground was difficult and included a number of steep banks and becks, private gardens backed onto the search area.

I remember stopping for lunch and discussing search possibilities for the afternoon along with other more trivial matters. After about a twenty minute break, we put our bags back on, ready to set off, at which point one of the Team announced, 'Here he is'.

We had been eating our lunch near a beck and tucked away right out of sight almost beside us, was our missing gentleman. He was very cold and confused but otherwise unhurt.

Quickly he was treated by our casualty carer and put into a casualty bag for warmth, before being loaded onto a stretcher for evacuation to the road and pick up by ambulance. The evacuation was of particular note because we had to find our way through someone's back garden and then negotiate their driveway past a very expensive looking BMW - unfortunately no one was home to ask for assistance.

Finding a quiet hollow around mid afternoon for a nap is very helpful. A chance to recharge the batteries for the effort of carrying a stretcher.
Chris Roberts

I'm not lost!

One Friday evening, sitting in my canoe on the River Tees at Barnard Castle coaching a group of youngsters from the Canoe Club, I noticed the Police helicopter fly overhead - something's going on I thought. Next I see the Team Control Vehicle race over the bridge - definitely something going on. I made my excuses and got back to the car to find that my pager was going like crazy.

We had a search for a missing walker on the Pennine Way.

I reached the farm where the search was centred, just West of Bowes. The Team had already established Control and groups were already out searching. I was a late arrival and was teamed up with a colleague to walk East back along the Pennine Way.

After a kilometre or so, we reached a farmyard with a gate. Coming towards us was a gentleman carrying a carrier bag who very kindly opened the gate for us. He politely informed us that this was part of the Pennine Way, to which we replied that we already knew this, as we were local and part of the Rescue Team.

We engaged in conversation and found out that he was camping in a field not far away, in fact, in the same field as our missing walker - and then, we established, the same tent - this was actually our man!

We pointed out several other search groups that were in sight and the Police helicopter that was flying overhead. 'But I'm not lost' insisted our gentleman, 'I've spent the day in Barnard Castle at the Bowes Museum, had a bit of lunch and a bit of supper and now I'm off back to my tent.'

The poor chap was very embarrassed by the whole episode and we assured him that there was clearly a misunderstanding and that he should not feel bad about the situation in any way.

It had just been a break down in communication. The farmer believed that our man was staying just one night, so when his tent was still there the next day without an occupant he became concerned and called police. The tent had been left in such a way that it suggested that the camper may have left intending to return very shortly. The fact he could not be found nearby suggested he may have walked away from the site and injured himself.

'Our man' was sure he had requested camping for two nights. All's well that ends well but I wont forget the words, 'But I'm not lost'.

Top Tip

Carry a camera, the bigger the better. Blokes are always impressed with size, even if you don't know how to use it - it's the same with cameras! Even if its batteries are flat, pretend to be David Bailey, it's much easier than lugging a bloody stretcher!
Scott Bisset

Do you believe in fate?

It was the October half term break and I was in Scotland walking the Cairngorms with a long standing walking companion. We had already had a couple of good mountain days, returning to Aviemore each evening but were now going on our usual 3 day walk into the hills. Our plan was to leave the car at Glenmore Lodge and head out for a first night at Hutchison Hut via Bynack More and Loch Avon (Loch A'an).

The weather was typical for the time of year with a mix of sun, rain and snow, and quite cold, particularly on the summits where it was freezing. We were in no great hurry, just enjoying being out on the hills.

At Loch Avon the weather decided to close in, the cloud came in and it started to rain, which then turned to snow flurries. Progress alongside the Loch was quite slow and when we got to the path that led up to the Saddle, Strath Nethy and back to Glenmore Lodge, we had a sit down and weighed up the options. With the weather closing in it wasn't going to be a particularly pleasant night out and if we turned off here we could be back for just after dark and into the pub.

First decision – we decided that we would carry on. We were well equipped, the weather wasn't so bad, and anyway we had a good bottle of malt to look forward to when we got to the hut.

As it was, shortly after leaving the stopping place the snow came down just that bit harder.

Second decision – rather than carry on to Hutchison Hut we decided to find the Shelter Stone and stay there for the night instead. Neither of us had stayed there before but by chance we had been talking to a fellow walker in the pub the night before and he had given us a good description of the place and how to find it.

The Shelter Stone is as it says on the tin; a stone that you shelter under. Well to be fair it's a great big boulder in a boulder field. It is propped up in such a way that it has a large space under it with a head room of about 4ft. Over the years it has been made weather proof around the edges so makes a pretty good bothy.

On the 25,000 scale map it is marked as a mountain refuge hut – something that would have an influence on what was to come. We found the Shelter Stone late in the afternoon – even in the light it's not the easiest of places to find. It was snowing on and off quite hard so we were pleased to get into the shelter and relative comfort. Once inside we got ourselves sorted. I had a low, easy to erect, mountain tent at the time, so put this up inside the space so as to give us that extra bit of insulation – something that was to cause some interest later.

We cooked and ate our meals, took what we thought was a last peek outside and decided to settle down for a night of idle chat accompanied by the bottle of malt.

Third decision – I'm not quite sure why, but we both thought we would just pop out for another look at the view before shutting out the elements for the night.

It was now just starting to get dark, the snow had stopped but there was a wind picking up. To the North, Cairngorm was rising up into the cloud and the dark. To the North West, Coire Domhain and … torch lights! Must be a group from Glenmore on night nav - What if they're heading here? Bugger – company is welcome sometimes, but in a small space it's not really what you want.

We went back in for shelter and chatted about who the mystery lights might belong to. If it was a training group, then they would probably pass us by. The route that the lights were coming down was not one you would expect.

We decided to go back outside and see what was going on. The lights were definitely coming our way. Like it or not, we were going to get company.

Remembering how difficult it was to find the shelter in the light, we put a lamp out to help guide the walkers to us, if this was where they were heading.

Progress was slow. The lights came and went. They got close but didn't seem to be making the progress that you might expect. At that point, Dave decided it was time to go and have a look and see if he could guide them in if needed.

A few minutes later, Dave appeared from behind the Shelter Stone. 'Chris we've got a bit of a problem here'. Memorable words!

He was supporting two exhausted young men and a third was in a state of collapse. I half carried, half dragged him into the shelter.

Once inside we started to get the story. They were out, like us, for a couple of nights in the mountains.

They had tried to put up tents somewhere on the tops but had been wiped out by the wind. They had looked at the map and seen 'mountain refuge hut' and decided that that was there only option. The climb down had been far harder than they expected. They had not eaten for some time because they had decided that going on was the best thing. They were wet and cold – due to exhaustion the third lad had stumbled into a stream making him very wet and even colder.

Dave took control of the two walking wounded and soon had them into warm clothes and a brew and food on the go. I was trying to sort out the other guy who was extremely cold and was not talking. I warmed him as best I could, in a sleeping bag and tried to get him to take some warm fluid. It was now about eight in the evening.

Our two walking wounded were getting more chatty and were making a good recovery – the third was not. He was still not talking, had not taken any food or drink and was clearly hypothermic.

Dave and I went out for a quiet chat. I was concerned that without help, we might have a death on our hands – we had to get help.

All three lads were now inside sleeping bags inside the tent under the Shelter Stone.

We had done all that we could there and decided that we must walk out and get help. We took details of the group – left them with instructions (Dave's parting words were, 'Don't touch my malt') and set off into the dark, wind and now snow.

The quickest route would have been to go up Coire Raibeirt to point 1141 and down to the Ski Centre but because of the worsening weather conditions, we decided on the longer but lower route up to The Saddle and down Strath Nethy, then along the forest track to Glenmore Lodge.

I have to admit that was the hardest, most stressful walk I have ever done. All the time, I was wondering how the guys were; had we made the right decision? We were both already tired and even though we wanted to push on we had to take occasional rests.

Once at Bynack Stable the path becomes obvious and firm. This was now familiar ground for us and I remember half running this last 3km stretch to Glenmore Lodge.

It must have been about 01.00 when we got to the Lodge – it had taken getting on for 5 hours to get back. Luckily there was a night porter on duty. The police and Mountain Rescue were called.

A team was assembled and flown by Sea King to the nearest landing site to the Shelter Stone.

Those words over the radio 'All three located alive and well' were just the best!

At about 03:00, there was the sound of the helicopter engine as the team returned to the Lodge + one casualty. Apparently, due to limited fuel and weight, our two more able lads had been left in the Shelter Stone. They were apparently fine and in good spirits and had agreed to walk out the next morning. 'Just better not touch the malt,' Dave was heard to mutter.

The kind people at Glenmore Lodge put us all up in comfortable beds and gave us a hearty breakfast. We didn't see our young man that morning as he was exhausted and fast asleep in his bed.

Dave and I? We had to walk back to the Shelter Stone to pick up all of our gear. As we walked up Cairngorm, we saw two figures in the distance coming down Coire Cas – our two we thought.

When we arrived back at the Shelter Stone, there was a guy sitting there having his lunch, listening to a transistor radio. 'There was a big rescue here last night,' he said. 'Can you believe it they put a tent up under the Shelter Stone.'

'Yes – we've just come to pick it up,' we replied – probably pretty smugly.

That evening we met up with the three lads and had a drink and a meal. They had done most things right but didn't have quite enough experience for the conditions. They had logged their planned route with the Rangers as is recommended. Had we not found them that night, they would not have been reported missing for three days – I fear that by then it would have been too late for all of them.

All of us that go into the hills put ourselves at some risk, which is probably one of the reasons why we do it. We can prepare ourselves for the mountains by learning the appropriate skills, but things can and do go wrong, even for the best prepared and equipped of us. Mountain Rescue is there for us when we most need them.

At the time this happened, I was just a Canoe Team member of the TWSMRT. Shortly after, I applied for full membership and the rest is history.

Of the three lads? – I have spoken to the boy that was helicoptered out once since. His mum has written a couple of times – she sent me a picture of his eighteenth birthday party, which was touching. He is now, I believe, a successful broadcaster.

Best still, Dave's malt was untouched – until the following night that is! So was it fate that made us change our plans that day?

Des Toward
Led astray

I sat in my local pub one night and I got talking to a fella who was walking the Pennine Way. A few shared pints later and I went off home. At three in the morning I was knocked out of bed to attend a callout, so I got up and joined the search.

It turned out the fella we were looking for, was the one I had spent the night in the pub talking to. Needless to say it was five years later before I actually admitted it to anyone!

It reminds me of a story that happened many years ago, to a fellow Member from the Northumberland Team. He got talking to a guy he met in the forest during a search. The guy asked him what he did and he told him they were searching for a missing man. The guy said, 'Oh, I'll help' and it turned out he was the man they were looking for.

Buried Alive

There was a callout to search for a missing man who was believed to have gone off to commit suicide. I worked one of the dogs for seven hours that day and eventually we came into a clearing in a forest. The dog began barking at the ground and all I could see was this white thing sticking out from the ground and I thought it was a big mushroom.

As I got closer, I realised it was actually a hand. It was the hand of the missing man.

He had dug himself a hole in the ground, put himself in it, then scraped the earth back over himself.

As we were putting on our gloves, he just sat up out of the shallow 'grave.' He wasn't actually dead at all.

I ran like fury and I think I said the 'F' word about 10 times – over the radio!

Top Tip

Don't eat yellow snow
or from my Norway training so many, many moons ago, don't eat any coloured snow, as it's likely to be bacteria and will most probably do you no good.
Also poo in a bag and seal it and use it as a hand warmer.
I have many others in the same vein, along with don't waste the heat of your wee…and three things to do with a sheep BEFORE you eat it - perhaps another time!!
Dave Wigham

Ian Findlay

Searching and rescuing people over the years is both sad and rewarding. Tragic accidents or incidents have to be treated with the utmost respect for the relatives and friends - it is also a sad time for Team Members.

A successful search for a missing person or group is both rewarding for relatives and Members. There are lighter moments which bring a smile to the face, here are a few of mine.

Bridal Trauma

The Team were called out to attend an incident involving a man with a broken ankle who had fallen from a small ledge of a cliff above the River Tees. It was a difficult rescue - evacuating by rope and stretcher and in all took 1.5 hours. The story behind the incident is this.

A party of 3 -4 men had been attending a stag night for the groom to be (the injured party) in a local pub and were invited back to a tent by a girl they had met there. The campsite was situated above the River Tees on the north bank.

Two of them began fighting for the attention of this young 'lady' as to which tent she should sleep in. During the fight both men fell over the cliff into the river. One of the men broke his ankle on a small ledge, the other swam the river and walked back across the bridge.

The callout came at 4.30 in the morning, the team arriving half an hour later. We were told the story at 7 - 7.30 am, and by then the bride-to-be of the injured man had arrived full of concern until she heard the full story - then went berserk. Despite the broken ankle he leapt off the stretcher and made for the cliff, only a quick thinking policeman stopped a second accident. This couple did not appreciate the funny side but the Team and the Police certainly did.

The law is to be followed as it is written, not your own interpretation of it.'
Advice given to me from some old judge bloke
David R

Thanks but no Thanks

A man was trapped on a ledge halfway up on the north side of High Force. It was difficult access. He was absolutely frozen with fear. The Team arrived with equipment and with much difficulty he was moved along the ledge to the water from the north side.

By then his confidence had returned and no way was he going to be hauled up quietly. On a given signal from me, we were hauled up through the light stream of water. At the top he was still ranting on. His girlfriend had arrived and was very pleased to see him safe. He demanded the car keys from her - snatched them and stormed off - without a word of thanks! Leaving us and the girlfriend gobsmacked - you win some, you lose some.

Phones

Following a callout to attend to a lady with a broken ankle, the team were harangued, bullied and threatened for not having suitable mobile phone reception in the area!. Despite explaining to her that mobile phones do not work in parts of the Fells, it was simply not accepted!

During a long stretcher carry out to the waiting ambulance both rescue and ambulance teams were subjected to a terrible tirade. My final remark to the lady was, 'If you are going to break a limb in these upland areas in the future, make sure you have a good mobile phone signal first'.

New Pastures

During the summer months, sheep, in looking for fresh grass, become crag fast on cliff faces and cannot get off. On being reported, they are often left 2 - 3 days to quieten down and then rescued by a rope. A steady quiet approach is essential and once secured by a sling around the horns and attached to the climbing harness, they are lowered to the cliff base. This rescue went according to plan, however one slight hitch occurred, with the abseil rope becoming snagged. This needed a stop to free the rope.

On looking down I was surprised to see the ewe 5ft below me who, despite being supported only by the sling around its horns, was happily tucking into a large clump of grass, this all 60 ft above the ground. Once free we carried on the descent to safety - the sheep equivalent to the 'Little Chef.'

Lucky Rescue

A golden lab called 'Sofie' tumbled and fell down the south side of High Force in pursuit of a rabbit. The Team were called out and the only access to the side was by rope. After expecting a serious injury it was quite a surprise to find only flesh wounds. I was licked to death by her, in the welcome of being rescued and reunited with her owners.

The owners of Sofie submitted the story of the rescue to a publication and on winning 1st prize, received £100. The Team also received a further £100 from the publication plus £25 from the owner.

The organisation I worked for, read about the incident in the local press. The internal newsletter released at a later date had the heading 'Ian seen hanging around High Force with Sofie!'

Top Tip

Carry a sit mat (bit of old Karrimat chopped off) - it makes sitting in group shelters and stopping for food etc so much warmer.

Izzy Barnes

Simon Stewart
Skye Rescue

Danny and myself had worked together for a long time before finding out that we had both been climbers and had both packed in due to not having a climbing partner or the spare time.

A climbing partnership was made and this had led us to the Cuillin Ridge on a wet, misty day slogging up the slopes of Scur nan Eag. We hadn't long left the lochain when a man appeared through the mist in front of us, 'Are you from Mountain Rescue?'

'No, what's wrong?'

'A chap has just fallen from the summit!'

With that he disappeared again into the mist. Without hesitation or even discussing it, we headed in the direction the man had came from and sure enough, before long, we came across the incident.

Joe, a man in his late seventies had fallen backwards off a block about eight foot high. He was with his mates, all of a similar age and was looking in good spirits despite the pain he must have been in. I ran up to the summit to get some reception on the phone and quickly got my grid reference sorted, 'Hello, can I have Mountain Rescue please, there has been an accident on Scur nan Eag'.

Youth Team recover casualty from earthquake training area in Iceland

The police officer said he would pass the info on to the Rescue Team and ring me back for more information. One of Joes' friends came up to me and he was able to give the information asked for, from the wife of the Team Leader. He was already on the hill guiding a party and the rest of the Team were making their way to Glenbrittle where they would be picked up by helicopter.

Top Tip

Ripe banana = quick release energy source
Green banana = slow release energy source
Packet of Rolos for a quick sugar fix
Midget gems for navigating for Paul R
Lenor fabric conditioner for re-proofing of Gore Tex kit,
its cheaper than the 'standard' re-proofer!!
Mark Davis

Joe was still in good spirits when we got back to him although becoming more quiet than before. He was sat up and well wrapped up with his back against a boulder for support. Joe told us he lived in Ambleside and he was on the hill with his friends every day. He was certainly fit for his age and the banter was that of good friends.

Before long the drone of the helicopter could be heard lower down the valley - the Team were dropped off near the site. We realised what was happening and a few of us set off down the scree to make a visual line of bodies to the incident site.

We were first met by a young man almost running - he was a medic, and then a steady stream of people, possibly not so fit, and mostly of the older generation carrying a stretcher and other bits of equipment.

We stood back from the scene and watched the team do their work, all knowing what each had to do. In no time at all, Joe was ready for transportation down the hill, not by helicopter but by manpower as the cloud was as thick as ever.

Gerry, the Team Leader, asked if we would help and we agreed to this instantly as the day had already been much more exciting than I'd thought it would be.

The plan was to take him down more or less the way we had come up, back to the lochen, where the helicopter could come in under the cloud.

Ropes were pulled from sacs and a body belay system set up. The rest of us were to carry the stretcher down the screes; where the going got tough, it was passed hand over hand and eventually the lochen came into view under the cloud.

A smoke flare was set off as the drone of the helicopter got louder and louder until it just appeared out of the cloud above us.

The winchman came down and after a short while both he and the stretcher were lifted away. Kit was put away and flasks and biscuits came out. We were given plenty of both and were thanked by the Team Members for our help.

'Would you like a lift back down in the helicopter?' we were asked - I was keen just for the ride, having never been in one before - but we had come to do the ridge and so we declined and started to make our way back up into the mist, just as the 'big bird' returned to take our new friends away.

We had lost our day. It had taken seven hours from when we had first met that man in the mist to now, but we had gained something much greater - the experience and memories that the mountains give you. You come across them by chance, given to you, they can't be taken, but just make sure you're prepared and have the skills and knowledge to make the most of the moment.

Top Tip

On overnight Bivvis have two plastic (carrier) bags with you
- one for each boot.
Whether you take your boots off or keep them on
it keeps the mud off your other gear.
Richard Glover

Canoe team training in the 1990's

Winter in the North Pennines

Teams Favourite Walks

Some of the Team Members have put together their favourite walks / bike rides and kayaking within the North East area. However, the Team stress that whichever walk you choose to do, be it a suggestion from this bunch or one of your own, taken from another source, then ensure you are always equipped with a map and compass, plan your route and always tell someone where you are going and the time you are expected home. Follow the country code, stay safe and enjoy.

David Bartles-Smith

Without wanting to sound anti-social, my favourite walks are usually the ones I do by myself - but I guess that is something many will understand.

Living in County Durham, we are fortunate to have so much choice. The Yorkshire Dales, North York Moors, Lakes and Northumberland hills are a day trip option, and a short weekend trip to the Scottish mountains is perfectly feasible too.

More often than not, I will be found somewhere in the Lakes or the North Pennines. The North Pennines offer something that for me is quite appealing. They are quiet, close by and will give you elevation and some quite breathtaking views. Not to mention the challenges in navigation and physical exertion. Perhaps they really are 'England's last wilderness!'

There is so much more to explore, please try it, you will be surprised and delighted.

Seasonal changes are marked. The winter storm on the High Pennine really can be akin to the Cairngorm plateau! Believe me - and long parched days in the summer bring a new challenge.

My favourite walk is so, because it takes you to an exceptional place and in combination with a mountain bike it can be a summer evening trip or a short half-day outing. The unfolding view as you ascend Mickle Fell (County Durham's highest peak at 788m) is, I feel, unrivalled. At the summit you look across to the Lakeland peaks, just a few miles away and South you take in the vistas of the Yorkshire Dales. Eastwards the lowlands of the North East spread out towards the North York Moors and North your view tops the Durham Dales towards the Cheviots on the Scottish Border, and just ahead the backbone of the North Pennines rolls up to Cross Fell at just under 3,000 ft.

Choose a day when there is a temperature inversion and you are in heaven!

Mickle Fell is a 3 km long plateau with a steeper southern edge. It is all above 750m, scree and small crag line the rim. You will also find the remains of a crashed aircraft if you look hard. Plenty to explore as you wander the plateau rim, sit, ponder, and admire the views!

Before you go however, you must check with the Warcop range – a search on any search engine or freephone 0800 783 5181 - this is an answer phone that tells you when there is access as this is an overshoot area for a firing range. Watch out for any munitions and please adhere to the country code and remember you are walking in a grouse managed area. The start of the route also passes through an SSSI - please read the access sign at the gate.

Park appropriately near the gate at Grid Reference 872212 on the B6276 from Middleton to Brough. A sometimes rough track will take you (and your mountain bike) westwards below Closehouse Crags and up to High Crag. The track has been extended from here and this will take you to a gate near the trig point at 758m.

Leave your bike here and walk the plateau to the summit at 788m. Stay and admire the views for as long as you wish. The return to your car on your bike can be very fast indeed - So take care! A brilliant wilderness trip when time is not on your side.

Youth Team on Snaefellsjokull glacier in Iceland

Stuart Kime (not a local walk)

My favourite walk is one that I've never quite managed to complete, but have enjoyed every time I've tried it. Just north of Crianlarich, past Tyndrum, is Achallader Farm. You can park there which is a bonus. The train line from Crianlarich runs up here, but there's no stop close by, although I've always wondered if the train goes slowly enough for an ad hoc exit mid-way along the line!

Walking East from the farm, following the track across the stream, you come to Gorton Bothy just over 10km in (the Mountain Bothies Association may discontinue my membership as a result of this admission!). From Gorton, the route goes south, under the train line (through a sheep creep) and up towards Ben Chruachan. On a good day, coming round from the north and up the west face of the mountain is a pretty good idea (so I'm told!) but I've been convinced for a while that picking a track up the north side of the corrie bowl is a good idea.

If the weather is fine, I think it is. On the occasions I've tried it, it hasn't been. The wind can be pretty stiff up there on a bad day and it's not a good place to discover how good your balance is! So, due to all kinds of rough weather and a general inkling that I'd like to hang around on Planet Earth a little longer, I've never got to the top of this Munro.

One day, I'm sure; I'll see what the world looks like from up there.

Izzy Barnes

I have a mountain bike ride, which I did recently and is definitely one of my favourites now. It is taken from the Beyond Hamsterley Guide Book though. It's from Cow Green to High Cup Nick and back along the Pennine way. It may sound a little dull doing a there and back route but it was fab.

You're supposed to walk from the car park to Cauldron Snout; for some reason cycling is not permitted. The ride to High Cup Nick is hard work, mostly gently uphill over rough terrain and, with the wind against us, especially hard work. Don't be ashamed if you have to walk some of it, or a lot of it. (See it could be my favourite walk too!)

Arriving at High Cup Nick though is of course spectacular and worth the effort. It was great weather the day we went, so we had a lovely time chilling out admiring the views, eating chocolate etc.

Then came the return, which is brilliant. Lots and lots of fast riding downhill taking half the time it took to get there. Despite being the Pennine Way there are never loads of walkers so we did not have to stop for anyone and didn't create any jobs for the Team by crashing into any of them! (Always good for a Team Member not to cause accidents!)

Being nice weather and the Pennine Way it was easy navigation which is ideal for bikers as the fun is ruined if you have to keep checking where you are. So all in all, a great day out combining the best things about the great outdoors - Challenge, excitement, wonderful scenery and loads of fun!

Young Chris Toward

Park at the Forest-in-Teesdale car park just off the B6277, head along the road in the direction of Langdon Beck. Roughly 100 metres along the road on the left hand side there will be a track towards a farmhouse, follow the track to the farm, then follow the footpath signs through the next three or four fields heading down towards the River Tees.

Use the bridge over the Tees, then continue following this track up the small hill towards Cronkley Farm (this can be singled out due to a newish looking large barn within its perimeter), walk into the farmyard and then follow the footpath signs towards a steep slope seemingly covered in juniper bushes and then follow the path through these.

At the top, the path meets a wall with a stile within it, once over this the footpath is marked by large slabs of stone, follow these as far as possible. Now the path yet again crosses another wall, follow the path up the small slope towards what is known by locals as the black barn, this is actually an old carriage that was used by grouse beaters to shelter in bad weather.

Before reaching this shed, the path turns right heading down towards a small gate within the wall, go through this taking caution because of the small beck, which often floods, continue on the right hand path until it joins a larger path. This new path will look like a large green track through the surrounding scenery.

Turn right following this path up towards what appears to be a steep fell side where the path cuts over from right to left, whilst going up this path there is only one piece of steep ground which, after much sweating and cursing you will come across a post depicting the land's access rights, from here you can see down the valley towards the fells above Middleton-in-Teesdale.

Follow the path over the large top of this fell observing the meshed fenced off areas on either side of the path; these contain the rare spring gentian and large amounts of sugar lime both of which are tormented by rabbits.

After wandering over the top you reach what seems to be a large spring with a natural bridge over it, from here you can see right up the Pennines over to Great Dunn, Cross Fell, and Tynedale etc. The path soon begins to descend back down towards the River Tees, the next junction of paths, which will be in the valley bottom, take the right hand path heading downstream back towards the start point.

Eventually after roughly 1 hour, the path comes to a small barn near to a conifer plantation, here follow the footpath signs into a large wide-open field. Follow the path/track through this, until it joins the track at the bridge, which was crossed earlier during the walk; from here follow the footpath, which firstly brought you here. Throughout this walk, there is a lot of rare wildlife and plant life to be seen, from the spring gentian and bird's eye primrose to the common lizard, and the rare red kites are often seen too.

John Little

There are a multitude of places to canoe and kayak in County Durham from the still and gently flowing sections of the River Wear, passing Durham Cathedral and Finchale Abbey, to the thundering waters of Cauldron Snout.

One of my favourite sections, after a little rain, starts at Stanhope stepping-stones and comes down the River Wear to Wolsingham. The river has almost continual interest with small (depending on your point of view!) rapids the whole way down.

There aren't usually any really hard sections and on either side of the river and glimpses of the area's industrial heritage can be spotted. Please check the latest access agreements before paddling.

One of my favourite cycle rides in the area is descending the Waskerley Way from Park Head Station down into Durham City. This is a fantastic ride of a little over 20 miles, which starts up on the tops of the Pennines and gently descends down through the industrial heart of Durham County finishing in the urban fringes.

Following the old railway tracks, this is almost completely off road and can be completed by a group of 8-year-old children in a little over two hours.

The tracks are well made and almost the entire route is down hill with just a few roads to cross. If you want a little more challenge, the section above Parkhead station from Dead Friars is also down hill but the ride is much more technical.

Ready for crowd surfing

Lorraine Allison (one of the partners)

Sunderland Bridge circular walk

This is a very pleasant 7-mile walk just outside Durham City. It includes woodland, riverside and field paths, which can sometimes be muddy in places.

Although only a stone's throw away from the City Centre I have seen deer, squirrels and a variety of bird life together with more domesticated Highland cattle, turkeys and the tiniest Shetland ponies kept at High Butterby and High Croxdale farms.

I have done this walk many times, as a whole and in sections, in good and inclement weather, always finding something new and interesting along the way.

As a bonus, there are two places to refresh one's self, the Garden Centre and The Seven Stars Pub both in Shincliffe.

Note

Grazing animals. Always keep dogs on a lead and follow the country code. Above all, enjoy.

The walk

Park at the end of Old Sunderland Bridge, grid reference NZ 265377 Walk through the large metal gates into the parkland. As you walk under the A167 the beautiful avenue of Sycamores come into view, one that I never tire of. Once over the cattle grid follow the path around to the right to reach Croxdale Hall, built 1760.

This is the seat of the Salvin family. It was used as a military hospital 1940-1945 and from 1945-1952 on a maternity hospital. Although still owned by the Salvins the Hall is not open to the public.

The path continues left, on the left is a 12th century chapel and straight in front a huge stone barn where my dog Berry and I once took shelter from a sudden downpour. Between the chapel and the barn the path continues left then right onto a surfaced lane, watch out for free range chickens!

After about 880yards you pass Croxdale Wood House on your left and Wood House Cottage on your right. Here the lane becomes an un-surfaced farm track with Butterby Wood on your left and good views to Thrislington Works on your right. The track continues to High Butterby Farm, an interesting organic farm that is home to Highland Cattle, Turkeys, Bees and Donkeys. Pass through the farm buildings where in the yard a yellow way mark (public footpath) directs you into Shincliffe Woods, which are managed by the Dean and Chapter of Durham Cathedral.

Go down the steps, which are fairly steep, to the banks of the river. It was around about this area, where in May 2008 Berry and I met a family from Sunderland with another red collie called Jack who now does agility with Berry.

In springtime, these woods are covered in wild garlic flowers and if you are quiet and lucky, you may see deer. Follow this wooded riverside path and where it ends, turn right away from the river. The path takes you to the woodland edge with Shincliffe Hall on your left. This Hall was until recently owned by Durham University's Graduate Society.

On leaving the wood, the tarmac lane takes you to Shincliffe Village first passing Poplar Tree Garden Centre on your left. This is about the half waypoint and a good place to stop for a well-earned cuppa.

From the garden centre, turn right into the village and if alcoholic refreshments are required the Seven Stars pub is at the end of the village on the left. Here you meet the busy A177, turn right and follow the road on the path side uphill.

At the Shincliffe by pass, cross the road to enter Strawberry Lane. The lane bends right, ignore this and enter left into a field. Follow the field edge and at the end look left for a gap in the hedge, go through this gap into a hedgerow lined path. Continue on this path crossing the farm road; go straight ahead into a field.

From the field continue into a small fir tree plantation. Continue looking to the right for a path, which crosses a plank bridge, it's always wet here. Cross the plank into a field, this takes you to High Croxdale Farm.

Pass the farm on your right and follow the lane, which takes you back to Croxdale Hall.

Early Team Land Rover - The one that got away

Icelandic exchange visit
thanks to LEADER+ funding

How we are funded

Financial Support

Perhaps the most important aspect of the Rescue Team's work is its constant efforts to finance its' operations. As a registered charity the Team is very much responsible for its own funding. This has become much harder as public demands on its' resources have increased.

However, far from restricting their operations to that of an ordinary Fell Rescue Team, its' members have risen to the challenge of raising more funds through increased commercial sponsorship and public donations year after year.

In its early years, fundraising was met with overwhelming support from the local community. The very first sponsored fell walk held by the organisation in 1969 saw over £850 collected in donations. This proved to be so successful that it became an annual event. Future walks attracted people throughout the local community, and even received support from high profile figures such as David Bellamy.

An official involved in one of these early events commented, 'The real success lay in the fact that such numbers of people from the urban areas demonstrated their awareness of the value of fell rescue activities by joining the many local walkers in supporting an organisation which serves both types of community.'

However, sometimes even fundraising could be interrupted by rescue operations. While supervising one sponsored walk in 1992, ten members of the team had to leave temporarily, to rescue a teenager who got into difficulties near High Force. The team administered first aid for a gash in the leg then stretchered him to safety.

Afterwards all the members simply went back to supervise the walk. All in a day's work for fell rescuers!

As the Team has expanded its' role to take part in rescues beyond the fells, to cover the whole of County Durham, its fundraising has had to evolve into that of a commercial organisation in order to gain grants and higher levels of sponsorship.

This new professionalism was reflected in one of the most important fundraising efforts that the Team carried out in its history. This was encompassed in a five year plan for the Base Appeal 2001 Project.

Attempts at casual fundraising were devised to fund the project but it was the Team's new professional approach that saw its long service to the community justly rewarded when it secured National Lottery Funding.

40 years of Funding - Chris Scott`

I have had contact with the team for 40 years and I thought I should make a small contribution to this publication. I took over as Team Treasurer in 1998; before me were Eric Richardson and Bert Pratchett, the only people to have held this post since the Team's inception. These stalwarts produced their annual reports by hand or duplicate on a typewriter using carbon copy paper and even more daunting for me, added up the figures manually! To compete with their standards I could only use my limited computing skills to produce the accounting statements.

What did I know of accounts? 'You will learn', Bert told me, and I certainly did.

To be fair, he summarised his experiences; 'Always pay by cheque and never use one lot of cash to pay for something else without banking it first'. Wise words and my only guidance until David Clark agreed to hold a watching brief.

Four computers later, I can see changes that have taken place, but how do I make it interesting? Perhaps a mass of spreadsheets, or reports, or graphs, or …

This is how I feel at each committee meeting - what do I say and how do I say it to avoid eyes glazing over. Numbers are boring but a brutally honest medium … perhaps I should start in 1968.

In that year, the first Team Land Rover cost £361, vehicle insurance was £43 and team insurance cost £27. The money was raised from a sponsored walk and sale of work. Compared to today (with the current Land Rover costing £30,000, the Control vehicle £37,000, vehicle and team insurances at £4,320) little money was needed.

It had to be found, though, and in 1972 the total income was only £59. In those early days, you would argue, correctly, there were very few callouts and therefore low overheads. In fact, I can not remember there being much 'over our head' at all; there was no rescue centre; the garage was a barn and most equipment was stored in Member's vehicles!

The current rescue centre, of which the Team is rightly proud, was completed in 2001 at a cost of £165,000. I know that £123,000 came from lottery funding but the remaining £42,000 was a huge fundraising task.

By comparison, the Team once kept its equipment in Barnard Castle, paying a rent of £1,000 per year for an office and 2 garages. The drying room was a rack suspended in the entrance and the garages had no heating at all.

Even earlier, in 1974, £500 saw us move into a wooden hut on land kindly donated by Raby Estates, at High Force. This became the equipment and vehicle store which, in the winters of those days, was a trek just to get there. I remember the Army getting a tracked personnel carrier snowbound nearby so it was never an ideal location.

Financing a successful charity is never easy; money is always needed for equipment and running costs. Few, outside the Team, realise that apart from V.A.T exemption on a very few specialised items, Central Government provide no funds. This means that only through the generosity of the public can the increasing costs of Search and Mountain Rescue be met.

Although the financial records are not quite complete, the public have given an amazing £624,000 in 40 years and the Team's continued survival is in their hands.

Members receive no payment for their time and it would be against the principles of this fine service if wages became the raison d'etre. Oh well, the next Street collection is on Saturday, I hope we take enough to buy fuel for the Land Rover!

Would you like to support the team?

Annual running costs of over £30,000 are met entirely by voluntary donations, grants, charitable trusts and sponsorship. The Team is a registered Charity (Charity number 508877). The Team consists of around 50 volunteers, all on call 24 hours a day, 365 days a year. All our volunteers have full time jobs and meet almost all their direct expenses of being in the Team. The Team will typically respond to between 40 and 50 requests for help every year.

Making a donation

Every donation is welcome - buying this book was one of them, so thank you. The Team qualifies for gift aid so donors can donate that extra bit more. If you want to gift aid a donation please complete and return our gift aid declaration form which is available from the website and you can also donate online using PayPal, or as the Team is registered with the Just Giving website, that may be a suitable alternative.

Sponsor a piece of equipment

In addition to general running costs the Team regularly purchase a wide range of equipment. Equipment costs range from a few pounds to many thousands so if you would like to sponsor a particular item of equipment please contact the fundraising officer whose details can be found on our website. These are just a number of ways in which you, the public can help and all support is gratefully received with many thanks.

Rigging for a dog rescue

Some Final Words

Alan Best

It has always been when the phone call comes in, or the pagers go off, that the strength of the Team is manifest. The desire to do the best possible job for the casualty or their relatives, often in the most adverse of condition, is the underlying powerful spirit that bond Team Members together. Sometimes Team Members witness the most harrowing of scenes at some incidents.

This is when the dry humour and wit with which a number of characters in the Team are gifted, keep even the worst of images in perspective. When there is the greatest camaraderie and support. It takes a wide range of character of the men and women in the Team for it to function well.

Hopefully it has become clear what a wide range of talent, skill and expertise go to make up the Team. The amount of time spent in reflection sharing ideas and training. The Team, to be successful, has to have its' core dedicated and determined Members not just when the Team is in action but those, secretary, treasurer, press officer who ensure the structure of the organisation is run efficiently and effectively.

All three of these roles, by the end of the 1990s, were in the hands of the most conscientious, committed and hard working individuals, Treasurer Chris Scott and Press Officer Steve Owers and finally someone who made one of the fullest commitments to the TWSRT, was Team Secretary, Stan White.

Stan worked tirelessly over many years in the Team and with NESRA. He must have been dogsbody for SARDA training more than anyone else. He hardly missed a callout where he became our Land Rover driver. Blunt when required, Stan didn't suffer fools but was the most reliable and dependable of individuals. He ensured the organisational cogs of the team ran smoothly. He was meticulous and efficient with boxes of records detailing callouts and Team business from the late 1980s.

Stan died suddenly at home in 2002. It was a tremendous blow to all who knew him; he was thought by many to be irreplaceable following his death, indeed his role had to be split into many parts, but Stan understood the strength of the Team and the role of the individual in it.

Dave Clarke was sorting through the wealth of information sent to us by Stan's family and came across this epitaph for us to find. It is a thought that a member of any team should perhaps bear in mind.

The indispensable man

Sometimes when you are feeling important,
Sometimes when the ego is in bloom,
Sometimes when you take it for granted,
That you're the only one qualified in the room.

Sometimes when you feel that you're going,
Would leave an unfillable hole,
Just follow these simple instructions,
And let them humble your sole.

Take a bucket and fill it with water,
Put your hand in up to your wrist,
Pull it out, the hole remaining,
Is a measure of how you'll be missed.

You can splash all you wish when you enter,
Stir up the water galore,
But stop then in no time,
It looks the same as before.

The moral of this quaint example,
Is do the best that you can,
Be proud of your achievements but remember,
there is no indispensable man.

Saxon White Kessinger

Team on excercise in Upper Weardale

Our Thanks and appreciation to RAF Rescue

Useful and Further Information

Mountain Rescue Council and mountain advice
www.mountain.rescue.org.uk

North East Search and Rescue Association (NESRA)
www.nesra.org.uk

National Search and Rescue Dog Association (NSARDA)
www.nsarda.org.uk

SARDA - England
www.sardaengland.org.uk

Mountain Weather Information Service
www.mwis.org.uk/areas.php

Met Office
www.metoffice.gov.uk/weather/uk

Explore Teesdale and find out about events, attractions and accommodation at
www.teesdalediscovery.com

Teesdale & Weardale Search & Mountain Rescue Team
www.twsmrt.org.uk

Barnard Castle Tourist Information
www.touruk.co.uk/county-durham/BarnardCastle.htm

North Pennines Information
www.northpennines.org.uk

Outdoor Activity Centre - Kingsway Adventure Centre
www.kingswaycentre.co.uk

Raby Castle
www.rabycastle.com

For further reading on some of the subjects covered in this book TWSMRT would recommend the following:
'Search Dog' written by Angela Locke
'Sam & Co' also by Angela Locke

RAF Rescue
www.raf.mod.uk

Dusk at Cow Green Reservoir - setting off a flare for the helicopter

What to take on the Hill

Safety Checklist

- Wear suitable clothing:
    - Warm layers with waterproof outer layer
    - Boots with good deep treads
    - Hat, gloves and spare clothing
    - Suncream may be required (if you are lucky)
- Rucksack - to carry food, a warm drink, a bivi bag, a luminous panel, a torch, personal first aid kit, map, compass and a whistle
- Check the weather forecast
- Leave details of your intended route and when you plan to be back
    – you may consider using the Team website **'My Trips'** link
- Plan your route and stick to the plan – if you have to change the plan, make sure the person with your intended plan is also updated
- Know where you are and how to give a grid reference
- Know what to do in an emergency – how to get hold of Mountain Rescue, keep warm and dry, use the whistle to attract attention (6 blasts every minute)
- Keep together – if absolutely necessary for someone to seek assistance, do not let them go for help by themselves or without a map and compass

In Winter

All of the above PLUS

- Wear winter weight boots and goggles
- Extra warm clothing is essential
- Make sure you have enough time and daylight
- Carry extra food
- Torch with spare bulb and battery
- It may be necessary to carry an ice axe and crampons
    – and know how and when to use them

This is a suggested list and by no means exhaustive – make sure you plan your route and stick to your plan – remember to take account of the slowest or least experienced member of your group when planning routes etc

APPRENTICES at Thorn Electrics, Spennymoor, have designed and built a life-saving invention.

They have come up with a motorised stretcher, powered by a lawn mower engine, for fell rescue.

The stretcher will be presented to the Chief Constable of Durham, Mr Arthur Puckering, vice-president of the Fell Rescue Association, tomorow.

Mr Puckering will receive the stretcher on behalf of the Tees and Wear fell rescue section.

Get fell in for rescue on wheels

The stretcher is mounted on a frame, fitted with wheels and geared to operate at around 3 mph.

List of Donors

Whilst every effort is made to acknowledge donations to the Team, there are many hundreds of people who have not been recognised in this list – classic examples are donations we receive at Street Collections, the many collection boxes that are strewn through the County, fundraising using the Just Giving site or indeed, you, Dear Reader, who has helped support our fundraising efforts

Our sincerest apologies if you have donated and have carried out a quick search of your name or group, but not found it

Donors

Mrs Sarah Barker

Bollihope Estate

Durham Police Authority

Durham University Charities Kommittee

Leader Plus Programme

Teesdale District Council

Lloyds TSB Foundation

Thomas William Suddick

Durham Shopping Extravaganza 2000

Mr Peter Bell

Awards for All

The Lord Barnard

Durham Police Authority

Foundation for Sport and the Arts

The Hon H. F. C. Vane

Prison Service Charity Fund

Mr Ben Blackett-Ord

Mr and Mrs J H V Walker

Dr John Little

The William Leech Charity

Glaxo Smith Kline

Stoneleigh Residential Home

Northumbrian Water PLC

Northern Electric PLC

The Sir James Knott Trust

Sea and Mud Fundraiser 2007

Mountain Rescue Council

County Durham and Darlington Fire Brigade

Dale View Caravan Park

North Pennines AONB Partnership

The Council of the City of Durham

Councillor David Armstrong

St Aidan's College

Century FM

William Webster Charitable Trust

Province of Durham Masonic Benevolent Cttee

R.A.O.B. Bishop Auckland & District PGL

Barnard Castle Meet Committee

Durham Constabulary Motor Cycle Section

Hamsterley Hoppings Committee

GO Country Club

Charity Payments Department

Mr Peter Elliott

Inner Wheel of Durham

Dales Community Alarm Trust

Mickleton and District Fun and Charity Events Group

Donors

County Durham Foundation

Hamsterley Vintage Collectors' Club

Durham Police Headquarters

Her Majesty's Prison Frankland

Durham City Young Farmers' Club

Bishop Auckland and Spennymoor Round Table

Durham City Council

Mr Stephen Carter

Mr Mark Binney

Mr Stephen Marrs

Mr D King

Railway Pensions Management Ltd

Miss Karen Fisher

Phoenix Walking Club

Roseberry Sports and Community College

Middleton in Teesdale Carnival Committee

Mrs J M Turnbull

Sunderland C. H. A. and H. F. Rambling Club

Weardale and District Motor Club

Inner Wheel Club of Barnard Castle

Quakers' Running Club

Mr Stephen Hutchinson

Mr Andy Downer

Mr Alan Best

Pearl Assurance Company

npower

Weardale Flower Club

Mr and Mrs Debbie and Cliff Allen

Pearl Assurance Company

The Rotary Club of Barnard Castle

Barnard Castle R A O B

The Clique

Mr Keith Rodway

Mr Scott Bisset

Stanhope Cricket and Sports Club

Mr Chris Roberts

Team Descend M2W

Mr and Mrs D and J M Johnson

Red Lion, Cotherstone

The Patricia and Donald Shepherd Charitable Trust

Mr Ian Andrew

Middleton in Teesdale and District Home Ambulance Scheme

North Eastern and Cumbrian Co-op

Mr Anthony Tubbs

St Mary's Church Masham

Abbey National PLC

Executive Languages

Teesdale Community Resources TCR

Barnard Castle Dog Training Club

Darlington Advanced Motorists

Darlington Inner Wheel Club

Mrs A E Thompson

Mr and Mrs FK Staley

Middleton Guides

Ryton Tri Club

The Rothley Trust

Mr Robin Laycock

Dr Cedric Scott

Glaxo Smith Kline

Mr Ken Saxby

Barnard Castle Methodist Church

Darlington C. H. A. and H. F. Rambling Club

Mrs Jean Ambrose

Mr Kenneth Grainger

Mr Eddie Todd

Mr and Mrs Ian and Ann Foreman

Environment Agency

Siemens P. L. C.

Langdon Beck Hotel

R. A. O. B.

Inner Wheel of Durham Bede

Miss Anne Richardson

Barnard Castle Group Ramblers Association

Teesdale District Council Sports and Social Club

Mr Ian R Stewart

Mr John Holmes

Mr and Mrs R Redfern

Mr Justin Hawgood

Merry Oaks Women's Institute

Mr Neville Wilkinson

Barnard Castle School

Mr Ian Bainbridge, Stephen and Dennis Marrs

Mr H Parkin

Countryside Agency

Glaxo Retired Staff Club

Mr Anthony McAdam

Mr Dennis Marrs

Teesdale Trefoil Guild

High Force Centre

St John the Evangelist Lynesack and St Mary Woodland

Medomsley PCC

Huntsman Tioxide

Wear Valley District Council

The de Clermont Charitable Company Limited

Darlington Borough Council

Mrs Margaret Colclough

Durham City Young Farmers' Club

Strathmoor Arms

Durham County Council

Rose and Crown Gardeners' Club

Mrs Isabella Barnes

Mr G T Wilson

Mr and Mrs A Thompson

St Edward's Fellwalkers

Mr Andrew Smyth

Mr and Mrs G and B Blake

Mrs K M Quilter

St Cuthbert's Primary School

Mr B Bolton

Mrs H Richmond

Mrs E Smith

Northumbria Long Distance Walkers Association

Inner Wheel Club of Hexham and Tynedale

Mr G D Jackson

Glaxo Staff Charity and Community Fund

BT Community Champions

Mrs J B Davis

Mr JRC Lupton

3 M UK Holdings PLC

Woodburn Nurseries

Mr Pete Burrows

Mr David J Ramsden

Bishop Auckland Glazing Company Ltd

Dalesong Music School

Montalbo Primary School

Andrew Curtis-Haigh Esq

Mr Richard Warne

Miss Janet Parker

University of the 3rd Age Darlington

Sedgefield Methodist Wives and Friends

Durham University Charities Kommittee

Sale of Notelets and keyrings

Mr M Hemingway

Kenton Utilities and Developments Ltd

Mrs Charlotte Davis

Mrs Helen North

Durham County Association of Women

Ms Gail Foster

Copeland School

Donors

Gainford Women's Institute

Middleton Plus

Boldron Women's Institute

Mr M Clark

Mr Ian Bainbridge

Mr Paul Green

Mr J L Bumby

Mrs J Luckhurst

Mr J B Siddle

Hunwick Primary School

Porsche Club GB

Ms Carole Fairrington

Ingleton C of E School

Mr Richard S Graham

Miss Judith Bainbridge

Ms Julie Atkinson

Mrs R Dinsmore

Consett Afternoon Women's Institute

Mr A T Wilson

Mrs Pauline Wilson

Mrs H M Armstrong   A/c1460205

Lanchester E P (Cont) Primary School

Mr SMW Bishop

Weardale Steel (Wolsingham) Ltd

Lanchester Methodist Wives and Friends

Sedgefield Borough Council

Dr AC Greville

Soroptimist International of Darlington District

Mrs Mary Phillips

Mrs Alma J Turner

Shildon Bowling Club

Mr Alan Whittaker

Douglas Heath Eves Charity

Ms Mary Fisher

Mrs H M Armstrong

Durham City District Cub Camps

G Granville

Eversheds LLP

Darlington Men's Forum

Mr Dave Myers

Mr Jonathan Roche

Ms Shirley Francis

Mr Andrew Tiplady

Kestral Medical Services

Mrs I Wilson

Travelcare

Mr William Beadnell

Ms Jenny Lodge

Mrs Eileen Rombach

Mrs A M Smith

St Paul's Church Badmington Club

Poplar Tree Garden Centre

University of the 3rd Age Washington

Shildon and Distict Flower Club

Woodland Luncheon Club

Taylor Woodrow Developments Ltd

Mr Trevor Allchurch

Mrs A Earl

South Stanley Junior School

S W Durham Training Ltd

Darlington Ramblers Association

Weardale Agricultural Society

British Cycling Federation

IT SS Curriculum Unit

Inner Wheel Club of Houghton-le-Spring

Mrs Gwen D Cowan

Barnard Castle Scottish Dancing Group

The Black Swan

Mrs Joyce Richardson

Coundon Primary School

Darlington Rucksack Club

Mrs J E Blewitt

Mr Ady Davis

Barnard Castle Ladies Contact Group

Mr Austin Dial

Simon Berry Optometrist

A and K M Billinge

Mr Fred Howells

St Andrews Ladies Guild

Mrs L Owers

Cotherstone 60 Club

Mr Jonathan Liddle

Mr A Johnson

Mrs M Warren

Mr Denis Coggins

St. John's Chapel Primary School

Mr C H Johnson

Bishop Auckland Evergreens

St. Mary's R. C. School

Miss Susan Swan

Ms J A Clough

Mr and Mrs A Cummings

Mr M Woodhill

Durham University Duke of Edinburgh Society

Durham Voluntary Countryside Ranger Service

Thankyou

'Final stage of dog rescue'

Youth Team
member
practising his
abseiling skills

Callouts

Once again, we have made every effort to provide a record of all the callouts the Team has been involved in over the past 40 years plus. It is highly likely that there are others that have been missed – and our apologies for that. If you would like to provide details of any rescue you are aware of that does not feature, please contact the Team.

Date	Description
0700 05/12/2009	07.00hrs Team placed on standby and Team Leader in planning discussons with Police in relation a vulnerable male missing in the Seaham area. Missing person turned up safe and well prior to deployment of search teams.
0850 24/11/2009	Team placed on standby due to the 130mm of rain that is expected to fall in the Hills around Keswick.
0815 22/11/2009	Request for Team to be placed on standby to assist further in Cumbria.
16.00 20/11/2009	16.00 hrs brief standby in relation to search for vulnerable male in Tow Law area. NOTSRT had agreed to assist as we had just returned from Cumbria floods. Quickly stood down as search not required following more information.
0300 20/11/2009	TWSMRT, already in the area dealing with a number incidents,joined forces with Swaledale, Kirkby Stephen & Keswick MRT to search for a missing Police Officer who was swpet away when a bridge collapsed. Search of rivers banks by Swift Water Technicians. "The body of a man, reportedly in police uniform, has been found in the search for PC Bill Barker, police said." (The Guardian Website) The body of Bill Barker was later discovered on the beach.
1145 19/11/2009	Team placed on Standby for 24 hous by Cumbria Police due to the high flood water in the region. Team stayed on standby until 2100hrs (19/11/09) and then called to assist Keswick MRT in the town of Keswick. Team assistd with a number of incidents in and around Keswick. Swaledale MRT and KSSMRT also in attendance.

1700
18/11/2009   Team member assisted at the scene of an RTC on A690 Durham. One male driver stablised using Mountain Rescue Casualty Care techniques prior to the arrival of emetgency Service.

1800
03/11/2009   18.00 hrs request by Police to assist in search for a male in the Chilton area of Co Durham. Search of farmland and deployment of 3 SARDA dogs. Nothing found and Team stood down at 23.30 hrs.

0900
24/10/2009   09.00 hrs further searches conducted with Team SARDA dogs in relation to ongoing search for elderly male missing from Ferryhill.

1950
22/10/2009   19.50 Team placed on standby to assist Swaledale MRT in search for 12 children lost on a hillwalk near Stang Forest. Team SARDA dogs deployed along with Team Landrover. Children found safe and well by Swaledale. Team landrover tasked assisted in evacuation.

0900
21/10/2009   09.00 hrs further searching for elderley male missing from Ferryhill. Assisted by Cleveland SRT and Swaledale MRT.

1500
19/10/2009   Search continuation of missing male from the Ferry Hill area. 10 Search Team members carried out a search of a dense part of woodland to the East of Ferryhill. Nothing Found. Investigation continues.

0900
17/10/2009   09.00 hrs search continues for missing male in Ferryhill. Daylight hours search conducted by Swaledale MRT and North of Tyne MRT, whilst we rested. RAF Seaking returned to assist. TWSMRT rejoined search at 16.00 hrs along with further support from Cleveland MRT. Search continued until 01.00 hrs the next day. An almost continuous 30 hour search by MRTs stood down with nothing found.

2030
16/10/2009   19.45 hrs request by Police to assist in search for eldeley male missing from home in Ferryhill. Search of urban areas, farmland and woddland. 18 Team members and two SARDA dogs searched until 05.00 hrs the next day. Assisted by RAF Seaking form RAF Boulmer. Nothing found. Search to be continued by Swaledale MRT and North of Tyne MRT

0835
26/09/2009   08.35 call out to attend rescue of male injured in quarry near Stanhope in Weardale. Air ambulance and Police helicopter also on scene. Casualty evacuated as Team arrive on scene.

2110
09/09/2009

21.20 call to rescue a female who was lying injured at the foot of a crag alongside the river wear in Stanhope. Fire and Ambulance Service also attended. Casualty recovered by Team using stretcher and ropes, and then handed casualty over to Ambulance Service.

1300
06/09/2009

13.00 Team whilst en route to previous incident came across a cyclist with possible serious leg injuries. Team members assisted on scene for an hour prior to the casualty being evacuated by air ambulance.

1215
06/09/2009

12.15 hrs Team requested to rescue a dog that had fallen down a cave shaft near Mickle Fell. Dog rescued from tight shaft by the Team.

2300
31/08/2009

Called by police after a report of a stabbing in woods near Chester-le-street. Two search dogs deployed but stood down after a couple of hours when nothing found and no report of anyone missing.

0230
24/08/2009

Called out at 0230hrs to search for 41 year old male in Bournemoor area, who was believed to be at very high risk of injury. Missing person found by a member of the public who alerted the Team who provided casualty care until county ambulance arrived.

2000
18/08/2009

Team member carried out a rescue from the River Wear at Durham after a male had fallen into the water. The team member stabilised the casualty in the water, no physical injuries other than the on onset of hypothermia. Casualty was extricated from the water with the assistance of the Fire & Rescue Service, Police & Ambulance Service.

1700
26/07/2009

17.00 very brief standby by Cumbria Ambulance Service to assist walker near Birkdale in Upper Teesdale. Team not deployed as Air Ambulance able to locate and evacuate.

2100
20/07/2009

Call out to search for missing female in the Consett area. River & woodland search. SARDA dogs and swiftwater technicians deployed and assisted by Police helicopter. Stood down at 02.00 hrs nothing found. Missing person turned up safe and well the next morning at 0530hrs.

1400
17/07/2009

14.00 hrs Team placed on standby by Police due to extensive flooding in the County. Stood down after 12 hours - Team not deployed.

1041
14/07/2009   Request by Police to assist in search for another missing male in the same area of the last search. HM Coastguard also involved. Body of missing person located and recovered by the Team

0845
12/07/2009   08.45 call out by Police to search for missing male in the Castle Eden Dene area of Peterlee. Police helicopter attended and HM Coastguard Teams searched shoreline. Body found and recovered by TWSMRT.

1642
07/07/2009   Team called to the Consett area to search for a lady missing from home since early morning. Missing person found safe and well by team member.

1800
27/06/2009   18.00 standby consultations with Swaledale MRT in respect of family of four lost in thick fog near Tan Hill Inn on Pennine Way. Located safe and well prior to arrival of MR Teams

1145
24/06/2009   11.45 call out to search for male missing in Weardale area. Stood down en route as person located.

2005
19/06/2009   Search for missing person in the Faverdale area of Darlington. Search team stood down at midnight, awaiting further information from the Police.

0950
29/05/2009   09.50 Police request Team to search terrain and river following report of a person threatening to jump from a viaduct - nothing found

1250
24/05/2009   Team member first on scene at car crash in Durham City. Casualty care given until County Ambulance arrived on scene.

0840
07/05/2009   Team member assists a 78yrs old lady who had fallen in Bishop Auckland she had bad cut to the head; ambulance crew took to Bishop Auckland hospital.

1515
19/04/2009   15.15 hrs Team member assisted as first on scene at a paraglider crash on Skiddaw. Keswick MRT and RAF Leeming MRT attended. Casualty evacuated by RAF Sea King with serious leg injuries.

0730
07/04/2009   Team called to Osmotherley (North Yorkshire) to assist Cleveland MRT in search. Missing person locate as team en-route.

03/04/2009	Team member came across member of the member of public who was in a despondent state. Team member looked after the casualty while waiting for county ambulance to arrive. Casualty transported to hospital by county ambulance.
0900 28/03/2009	09.00 Team continue search for missing female in York.
1201 26/03/2009	Team member assisted an elderly male with a heart problem following a car crash in Bishop Auckland until the County Ambulance attended.

0800
26/03/2009

*********Press Release********

Teesdale & Weardale Search & Mountain Rescue Team were one of five mountain rescue teams from the North East involved in the search for missing York chef Claudia Lawrence. Miss Lawrence, 35 was last seen more than a week ago in York. Sixty five mountain rescue team volunteers from Teesdale, Swaledale, Northumberland, Scarborough and Cleveland spent today (Thursday) searching land along the route between Claudia's home and her work at York University. Dave Bartles-Smith leader of the Teesdale Team said "In the past our search skills were predominantly used in upland areas. However in the past few years these skills have been successfully adapted to searching in lowland areas".

10.50 16/03/2009	10.50 request by Police to assist following report of a person on a bridge parapet over the River Wear. Initial police search with dogs and helicopter and deployment of Team swiftwater technicians.
2312 14/03/2009	23.00 call out to assist Swaledale MRT in search for two missing children. Searched through the night assisted by RAF Sea King and supported by additional resources from SARDA, Cleveland SRT, Kirby Stephen SMRT, North of Tyne SRT and Northumberland MRT. Boys located safe in search area as second phase started the next morning.
09.30 20/02/2009	09.30 hrs standby request to assist Cleveland SRT. Team not deployed as missing person located soon after standby request.
1700 12/02/2009	Team called by police at 1700hrs to search for missing female from the Fishburn Area after during winter storms. Over 130 hours of searching carried out. Missing person located safe & well.
10.00 02/02/2009	Team placed on standby by Police during continued blizzards.

1300
31/01/2009

Team Member in Lochnagar, Cairngorms assisted climber who had fallen approx 50m on 45° ice /snow before eventually self arresting with axe.

2000
29/01/2009

18.30 hrs Team SARDA dogs Skye & Holly) respond to assist Scarborough and Ryedale MRT in search for missing child.

00.20
29/01/2009

00.20 hrs request by Police to assist two Police Officers and a member of the public snowbound on one of the areas high level roads at almost 2,000 ft. Three Team members and Team Land Rover attended and recovered personnel and vehicles.

1730
25/01/2009

17.30 male with young children snowbound near Tan Hill - concern was they were unsure where they were and may have gone off road - India 55 located and police 4x4 able to recover - initial plan in place with TWSMRT and SMRT - Team stood down prior to mobilisation

1030
25/01/2009

Request from police to help evacuate a male with a broken leg & Hypothermia from the River Derwent near Allensford Country Park. Injured male airlifted to hospital prior to team being mobilised.

0130
25/01/2009

Teesdale & Weardale Search & Mountain Rescue Team have been coordinating a search overnight for a man missing from home in Easington Colliery, County Durham. The middle aged man was last seen when he left his home at 1.30pm Saturday and did not return. The Teesdale & Weardale team and the police searched the area around Easington Colliery overnight in driving rain. When the man had not been found by first light mountain rescue teams from Cleveland, Northumberland and Swaledale were called in to assist. More than 50 mountain rescue volunteers with 5 mountain rescue search dogs with police support expanded the search area at first light. At around 11.30 am the Police helicopter picked up a heat source and within a few minutes a mountain rescue team located the missing man near a stream to the south of Easington Colliery. The man was airlifted by the police helicopter to a waiting ambulance where he was taken to Hartlepool General Hospital. Dave Bartles Smith Weardale & Teesdale team leader said "This is the second major search we have been involved in this week. On both occasions the mountain rescue community came together to deliver a successful outcome. It is gratifying to know that volunteers will freely give up there time and travel many miles out of their own area in order to search for missing people."

2330
19/01/2009

A LONE fell walker from London was dramatically rescued from the highest point in the Pennines about 9 a.m. this morning after an all-night search by fell rescue volunteers The alarm was raised by the man's family about 11.30 p.m. last night when he failed to reach an agreed point on his hike along the Pennine Way. More than 50 search and rescue volunteers from teams in Durham, Cumbria, Swaledale, Cleveland and Northumbria were mobilised and snow clearing crews from Durham County Council were call out to clear roads in the Langdale Beck area to allow the search to begin. The police helicopter and an RAF helicopter were also involved. The search teams on the ground were hampered by freezing conditions and snow drifts up to five feet deep. The walker was located at 9 a.m. this morning after he was able to get out a call on his mobile phone. He was airlifted out of a point near Cross Fell, the highest point on the Pennines and taken to Cumbria. He is not thought to be injured.

0900
21/12/2008

0900hrs request by Swaledale MRT for Team assistance in search for missing person. Ten team members a two search dog's (Skye and N.U.T) attended. Teesdale foot team located the body of the missing person on the dam wall around 1200hrs. The body was retrieved by police divers and assisted by both Swale and Teesdale team members.

1712
20/12/2008

Team Search dog Skye was called to assist Swaledale MRT to search for a missing male for the Leighton area, Concern for the missing 22 year olds wellbeing was raised by family. Immediate search of the area where the missing male's car was located. Swaledale MRT after four hours of searching & nothing found it was decided to start at 0800hrs the following morning with additional personnel from TWSMRT, Upper Warthdale MRT and Search dog's.

0800
19/12/2008

Teesdale & Weardale Search & Mountain Rescue Team have been carrying out a search overnight for a missing 81 year old man. The gentleman was last see at his home in Stanhope Co. Durham just after lunch yesterday. (Thursday). 19 Rescue Team volunteers and 3 mountain rescue search dogs searched for 8 hours last night assisted by police officers and the air support unit. The search recommences at first light with the assistance of neighbouring mountain rescue team. Stephen Marrs Rescue Team Controller said "We had started to go over ground searched during the night and expand our search with the help of the Cleveland Team when a friend of the gentleman's family found him close to a quarry to the North of the town. We were able to get one of our medics to the scene within a few minutes. We decided that the safest option was to carry the gentleman to the Police helicopter which had landed 200m from the scene. Because of a steep slope we were assisted by a number of police officers and an ambulance crew. The man was taken to James Cook hospital by the police helicopter".

1828
18/12/2008

Teesdale & Weardale Search & Mountain Rescue Team are coordinating a major search for an elderly man missing from the Stanhope area of County Durham. The 81 year old gentleman was last seen just after lunch on Thursday. Overnight 19 members of the Teesdale & Weardale team worked with 3 mountain rescue search dogs, police officers and police air support to search areas to the north of the town. Team spokesman Steve Owers said " We found no sign on the man overnight so we will be expanding our search today (Friday). We have asked for assistance from all of the North East Mountain Rescue Teams so we can cover the extensive fell and quarry areas close to Stanhope".

0135
17/12/2008   Team requested to assist in search for missing child in the Ferryhill area. Child found safe
                  and well by the Police as Team members were en route to the incident.

04.00
04/12/2008   04.00 hrs Team 4x4 capacity on standby during heavy snowfall. Stood down at
                  12.00hrs.

1205
14/11/2008   12.00hrs Consultation by Police with Team leader on search for a missing male. Initial
                  strategies identified in these discussions lead to finding of the male by Police.

17.00
30/09/2008   Teesdale & Weardale Search & Mountain Rescue Team were called out this evening
                  (Tuesday) to search for a missing woman. The middle aged woman from the Crook area
                  went missing around lunchtime. Her car was found on remote moorland track to the north
                  of Hamsterley Forest in County Durham at 5pm. Fifteen mountain rescue volunteers,
                  three mountain rescue search dogs, six police officers and the police helicopter were
                  involved in the search. Steve Owers Rescue Team spokesman said "We started the
                  search just as darkness was falling. As the evening went on we finally were able to make
                  contact with the lady on her mobile phone. She was unable to tell us her location so it
                  took 15-20 minutes of talking to her and asking her various questions to try and establish
                  a rough search area. We were able to use the police helicopter as a reference point and
                  ask her to describe where she was in relation to the aircraft. We then sent out a search
                  group and we found her within a few minutes at around 8pm". The woman was then
                  taken to hospital by ambulance.

1200
28/09/2008   Assisted crag fast family group up the scramble at the end of Sharp Edge. Two male &
                  one female

1700
27/09/2008   The Team was asked by the RSPCA and Fire & Rescue Service to assist in the rescue
                  of a young Harris Hawk stuck in a tree. Three team members attended. The bird
                  eventually flew down to safety.

20.30
24/09/2008   20.30 hrs request by Police to search area next to Hury Reservoir following possible
                  sighting in relation to missing person incident yesterday (44-2007/2008) in nearby
                  Cumbria. Police helicopter and small search group with 1 SARDA dog attended.
                  Nothing found.

1700
23/09/2008   Search dog (Skye) was called to assist a neighbouring team (Kirby Stephen Mountain
                  Rescue Team) to search for a missing person in the Tan Hill area. They were stood down
                  around 2200hrs, the search has continued today (24th Sep) with several teams being
                  called in to assist.

12.30 05/09/2008	12.45 hrs Request by Police to assist in search for a grouse beater lost and injured. Location uncertain and eventually thought to be in Allenheads area, incident then transferred to NOTSRT.
12.45 03/09/2008	12.45 hrs request by Police to assist in search for missing male in Tow Law area. Body of missing person located early in search.
0715 14/08/2008	Team called by Police to assist in MFH search in the West Auckland Area. Missing person located by Police out of the area.
1600 05/07/2008	16.00 request by Police to assist in search for missing male in Waldridge Fell area. Search strategy given and SARDA dogs alerted. Stood down when person found safe by Police following initial strategy actions.
22.15 03/07/2008	22.15 Team member assisted at scene of motorcycle RTA in Weardale.
18.00 25/06/2008	18.00 hrs Request by Police to search for two elderly hill walkers reported overdue from walk on Cronkley Fell. Team assembling to start search when both walkers turned up safe and well.
21.44 23/06/2008	21.40 hrs request by Police to locate and evacuate injured female hill walker at the Stang Forest. Located on high ground some 3 km from public road. Evacuated to County Ambulance.
11.30 23/06/2008	11.30 hrs request by police to assist in evacuation of an injured male who had fallen down steep ground near at Ferryhill. Air ambulance also in attendance. Team utilised rope rescue techniques to evacuate male to County ambulance.
21.45 22/06/2008	Team SARDA dog responded to request from Swaledale MRT to assist in search near Leyburn. Stood down en route.
14.00 22/06/2008	14.00 hrs - request for assistance from Penrith MRT, following 999 call reporting a mountain biker being lost on Cross Fell plateau in very poor conditions. Team mobile and search group deployed and all bikers located safe and well having made their own way off the hill.

13.30
22/06/2008   13.30 hrs request by Police to assist in search for missing vulnerable male near Durham City. Search of woodland and farmland. Three Team SARDA dogs also deployed. Person found safe by SARDA dog.

2235
21/06/2008   22.35 request by Police to assist in search for missing vulnerable female in Durham City area. Initial search concluded by two Team members and SARDA dog, prior to the person being located safe and well elsewhere. Stood down 00.45 hrs.

12.35
15/06/2008   12.35 hrs request by Police to assist in search for missing male in the Beamish area. Search of woodland, assisted by Police helicopter and deployment of SARDA dogs. Missing person turned up safe and well as search was progressing.

00.25
15/06/2008   00.25 hrs request by Police to attend incident of male reported to have fallen 60 ft at Holwick Crags. Team en route when stood down as male located and walked out.

1816
13/05/2008   FIRST FIND FOR SARDA SEARCH DOG HOLLY, 42 year old male missing from home from the Byker Area of Newcastle. Mobile phone "Pinged" in the Chester-Le-Street Area. Police Air Support, 15 Mountain Rescue Team Members and 3 SARDA search Dogs assisted in the search. MFH found safe & well by Team SARDA dog in the Plawsworth Area of Chester-Le-Street.

0430
08/05/2008   Team called by police to search for missing female at 0430hrs this morning. Search of open ground and woodland. Assisted by Swaledale MRT and one SARDA dog. Police helicopter in attendance. Stood down at 10.00 hours - nothing found

2020
07/05/2008   Search for MFH elderly male in the Bowburn Area of Durham. Search teams along with SARDA Search dogs, police and Police helicopter searched the immediate area. Elderly Male found by Police in early hours of the morning in nearby Industrial Area.

1800
07/05/2008   Search Team members along with SARDA Search Dogs and Swift Water Team searched river after a report to the police of a discovery of clothing and 3 inflatable boats near a Weir on the River at Witton Park. Police helicopter in attendance. Nothing Found

1030
02/05/2008   Search continuation from 30/04/08. Searching for MFH 48 year old male from the Langley Park area of Durham. 343hrs of searching with the assistance from 4 SARDA search dogs. One Search dog from Swaledale.

2200
30/04/2008   Search for MFH 48 year old male from Langley Park. Search of local paths, tracks and wooded areas. Nothing Found. Search to continue tomorrow.

1638
30/04/2008

16.30 hrs request by Police. 2 Walkers rescued from Holwick Fell after sustaining injury when crossing small stream. Air ambulance was requested to assist and evacuate injured male, whilst female partner was assisted from fell by SARDA Dog Des and Team. Weather: localised rainstorms.

00.05
28/04/2008

00.05 hrs request by Police to search for person missing and distressed on fells near Tan Hill. Kirby Stephen MRT and Swaledale MRT also attended. 5 SARDA dogs deployed. Stood down as early searches commenced when person located by Police.

17:30
26/04/2008

Saturday 26th April 1730hrs two team members were about to start climbing at Castle Crag in the Lake District when they received a call from another search dog handler, who knew they were in the area, requesting their assistance in the search of 6 missing walkers in Wet saddle area of Shap who had became lost due to falling mist. The two members and Search dog Skye met up with Kirby Stephens MRT when they received a phone call from the police saying the missing party had re-located themselves and they no-longer required Mountain Rescue, it was decided that Search dog Skye and Search dog N.U.T with navigator Simon Stuart would walk up to meet the missing party. The party was never met and it was believed they got themselves down off the hill.

1030
17/04/2008

Team's Search and Rescue Dogs (Search Dog Skye and Search Dog N.U.T) were called to assist Cleveland Search and Rescue Team to search for a vulnerable 52 year old male from Manchester. The vulnerable male had left his van parked in the car park of the Sun Inn near Chop Gate North Yorkshire. The two dog teams were tasked to search wood land areas along with neighbouring search dog Molly from Swaledale Mountain Rescue Team. The missing male was located by a search group from a neighbouring team Scarborough & Ryedale Mountain Rescue Team who were assisting in search.

0900
13/04/2008

Search Continuation for missing male in the Middleton Tyas Area.

1030
12/04/2008

Ongoing Search. 3 SARDA search dogs with handlers assisting Swaledale MRT in the Middleton Tyas Area

1640
08/04/2008

1640hrs - Team's Search dogs were called to assist Cleveland SRT in locating a possible injured person crying for help (reported by a couple of fell walkers) Cleveland requested the assistance of the team's dogs as well as an RAF helicopter after a search by the helicopter turned up nothing. It was decided to stand down the dogs 19.35hrs

2120
07/04/2008

21:20hrs the team's Search and Rescue dogs were called out by NNPMRT to help locate 3 missing walker lost on the Cheviot. The dogs were stood down on route when the missing party was located by an RAF Sea King flying out of RAF Boulmer.

18.15
02/04/2008

18.15 hrs Police request Team assistance in search for missing person near Durham City. Team leader attending, when person located. Stood down.

2230
28/03/2008

Teesdale & Weardale Search & Mountain Rescue Team where called out at approx 22:30 hrs to assist the ambulance service in the recovery of an injured man. The man had been a member of a party of school children on an evening walk near the hamlet of Ettersgill near High Force in Upper Teesdale Co. Durham. Eight of our Team members attended the incident. The school party were led safely back to the outdoor centre where they were staying by other leaders within their group.

1500
23/03/2008

Teesdale & Weardale Search & Mountain Rescue Team where called out today (Sunday) at 15:00hrs to assist in the recovery of an injured man. The man had been walking with his family towards Gibsons Cave a popular beauty spot near Bowlees in Upper Teesdale, County Durham. Chris Roberts, Deputy Team Leader said "the man was apparently walking along the path when he slipped and possibly fractured his lower leg. An ambulance from Barnard Castle and the Great North Air Ambulance originally attended but the man was some distance from either the ambulance or the helicopter. Eight of our team members assisted the ambulance service in carrying the patient approx half a mile along the path back to the Bowlees car park where he was transferred to the ambulance and taken to hospital. The weather at the time was heavy snow showers but this did not delay the recovery.

16.25
22/02/2008

16.25 brief standby to assist Swaledale MRT in search for missing hill walkers near Tan Hill. Team SARDA dogs en route when persons located safe and well during initial response. KSMRT also on standby.

0900
16/02/2008

09.30 hrs canoe search of River Tees in Darlington area for missing male. Nothing found

0900
03/02/2008

Continuation of search for missing male on fells in Weardale. Day long search assisted by NNPMRT, NoTSRT, Swaledale MRT and 4 SARDA dogs. Search of open fell. Nothing found.

1345
01/02/2008

The Team were called at 1.45 pm to recover stranded drivers from vehicles stuck in snow on the A66 between Bowes and Penrith. 10 team members plus a vehicle from Deepdale Off Road ferried motorists from their vehicles to a reception centre set up at Bowes village hall. We were assisted by Swaledale MRT in working west from Bowes. Kirby Stephen MRT was working east from Penrith. The two MR teams met up at 5.45pm. Once the A66 was cleared teams checked the minor roads and the B6276 from Brough to Middleton in Teesdale.

2145
30/01/2008   Extensive search of high moorland location in very poor weather for Male missing
                      from home.

10.00
25/01/2008   10.00 standby and consultation with Police re: possible search in Darlington area, using
                      SARDA dogs. Dogs not deployed.

15.30
19/01/2008   15.30 hrs request by Police to assist in search for missing child. Team en route when
                      stood down as child found safe and well.

10.00
18/01/2008   10.00 search continues from yesterday. Team canoe group deployed alongside police
                      underwater unit. Nothing found.

1100
17/01/2008   10.30 hrs request by Police to search for person believed to have fallen into river at
                      Bishop Auckland. Search using Team SARDA dog, TWSMRT canoe group and Team
                      swiftwater technicians. Police underwater unit and Police helicopter also attended. Stood
                      down at dark - nothing found

08.45
07/01/2008   Team called to assist police.

16.30
21/12/2007   16.30 hrs request by Police to search for missing vulnerable male in Blackhall area. Three
                      SARDA dogs deployed along with Team search control. Search of coastal fringe
                      alongside HM Coastguard search teams. Nothing found.

17.45
06/12/2007   17.45hrs request by Police to assist in search of woodland in Teesdale following reports
                      of screaming. Police helicopter in attendance. Local Team members and 1 SARDA dog
                      deployed. Stood down once concluded this was a false alarm with good intent.

08.30
05/12/2007   08.30 consultations with Team leader by Police in respect of search for elderly male
                      MFH- no further action by TWSMRT at this stage.

16.00
17/11/2007   16.00 hrs request by Police to search for missing vulnerable girl in Stanley Co Durham.
                      Search commencing when she was located safe several km distant. Team then returned
                      to scheduled all night training exercise in the North Pennines.

1345
28/10/2007   Team member came across an estate car with two male occupants stuck in Stanhope
                      Ford with the river in spate condition. Accessed the ford from far side using 4x4 and
                      attached tow rope. Recovered vehicle and occupants back to Stanhope side to await
                      recovery of their vehicle.

19:04
28/10/2007   Team called by police to search for male missing from home in the Durham / Chester Le
                    Street Area. Mobile phone signal used to narrow down search area of missing male.
                    Team stood down to allow police to make further enquiries.

08.00
24/10/2007   08.00 hrs Team placed on standby in relation to possible search in Seaham area for
                    missing male. Stood down after person located safe by Police

11.00
12/10/2007   11.00 hrs request by Police to recover body of male from difficult ground under Hownsgill
                    Viaduct. 6 Team members completed recovery.

19.30
08/10/2007   19.30 hrs request by Police to assist with search dogs in wooded area near Durham City,
                    in relation to ongoing enquiry. Strategy discussed and two Team SARDA dogs deployed.
                    Nothing found.

04.00
30/09/2007   04.00 hrs Team SARDA dog deployed to assist Swaledale MRT in search for missing
                    soldier on exercise. 06.15 hrs Team placed on standby and called out at 07.15 to assist.
                    Stood down almost immediately when soldier was located safe and well.

2040
27/09/2007   22.40 hrs consultation by Police with Team leader in respect of two young missing
                    children. Children found safe by Police.

19.25
23/09/2007   Standby to assist Northumberland search teams. Team not deployed as person located
                    by Police.

01.00
19/09/2007   Two Team SARDA dogs assisted Northumberland National Parks MRT in search in
                    Newcastle area.

1900
16/09/2007   Team member assisted 2 casualties that were involved in a 2 car RTC. Team member
                    carried out Cas Care. Casualties treated for minor injuries.

1745
16/09/2007   Team vehicles with 4 team members travelling back from Team Exercise came across a
                    RTC. Team vehicles positioned to control traffic and 2 young people assisted out of
                    vehicle and kept warm in team vehicle, 3rd casualty immobilised in her vehicle and "C"
                    collar fitted, extracted when county ambulance and Police arrived on scene.

1300
26/08/2007   2 Team members whilst out training assisted in the rescue of a man cragfast from a steep
                    gully - Red Screes - Honister- Lake District.

12.30
24/08/2007   12.45 hrs request by Police to recover body of male, with gunshot wounds, from a fell
                side in Weardale.

13.00
19/08/2007   13.00 standby request from Swaledale MRT to assist in search for missing hill party in
                Tan Hill area. Kirby Stephen MRT also on standby. Two Team SARDA dogs sent ahead.
                Stood down when group turned up safe. Weather cold, wet and poor visibility.

20.30
17/08/2007   20.30 hrs two Team SARDA dogs deployed to assist Northumberland National Parks
                MRT in search for missing female. Stood down on arrival as person located.

0800
06/08/2007   Continuing search for missing farmer near Gibside. Canoe Search Team deployed to
                search River Derwent. Missing person found as part of the wider search operation.

2035
05/08/2007   Consultation with police as to the best way to gain access to the top of Cauldron Snout
                and the Dam Wall. Two elderly walkers had become separated whilst trying to raise help
                as their dog had injured itself.

2000
05/08/2007   Team requested to help North of Tyne and Northumberland National Parks Mountain
                Rescue Teams in search for missing farmer near Gibside, Burnopfield.

02/08/2007   Team SARDA dog requested to help in Search in Northumberland

2200
17/07/2007   23.00 hrs two Team SARDA dogs deployed to assist Northumberland NP MRT and
                North of Tyne SRT in search for elderly male missing in Tyne and Wear.

1815
15/07/2007   Team members returning from exercise assisted driver and passengers stuck at
                Stanhope Ford, Co Durham.

16.15
12/07/2007   16.15 hrs request by Police to search for missing vulnerable male in the Peterlee area.
                Steep gorges and wooded Denes. Two Team SARDA dogs deployed, with support from
                Police helicopter. Search about to commence when person located safe by Police
                outside of area.

11.45
10/07/2007   11.45 hrs brief standby to assist Northumberland National Park MRT and North Of Tyne
                SRT in search from missing male. Team not deployed as person located.

20.35 06/07/2007	20.35 hrs Request by Police for assistance following report of a 13 year old girl lost and distressed in steep wooded ravines of Castle Eden Dene. Team placed on standby, SARDA dog en route when Police helicopter located girl.
0040 01/07/2007	0130hrs Request by Police to assist in search for a vulnerable teenager from the Chester Le Street area. Missing person found in South Shields as the SARDA handler was commencing his search.
0315 24/06/2007	03.15 hrs. Urban rescue request by Police to assist in evacuation of an injured male from scaffolding. Fire service and ambulance in attendance. Casualty evacuated onto attending Fire Service Arial Ladder Platform.
23.55 18/06/2007	23.55 hrs brief standby to assist NNPMRT with SARDA dogs in search for missing vulnerable male in Northumberland. No further involvement.
07.30 16/06/2007	07.30 hrs continuation of search for missing soldier. Search involved NESRA MRT Teams with the support of military and the Police. Team SARDA dogs also attended. Body of soldier located by a Teesdale and Weardale SMRT search group.
1100 15/06/2007	12.15 hrs request by Swaledale MRT to assist in search for 17 year old soldier missing in swollen stream. Search of flood corridor and surrounding terrain. SARDA dogs, RAF Leeming MRT and RAF helicopters also deployed alongside military and Police. Search stood down at 22.00 hrs to recommence at first light.
0930 11/06/2007	09.30 hrs request by Police to search for missing vulnerable male in the Shildon, Brusselton Woods area. Two Team SARDA dogs deployed with Team support and assisted by Police helicopter and Police resources. Nothing found.
2000 26/05/2007	Team search dogs put on standby to assist NNPMRT & NoT for an on going search at Alnwick Gardens in Northumberland for a missing 70 yr old female. The missing woman was found safe SARDA handlers were being briefed.
1615 20/05/2007	Northumbria police via NNPMRT/NOTSRT requested Teesdale to be on stand-by then called to assist in a missing person search in Chopwell woods. TWSMRT were training with RAF Helicopter in Teesdale, and a search group and SARDA dog were flown to search area. RAF conducted aerial search. As ground searches commenced - the missing person was located by Police outside of search area.

18.15 06/05/2007	Team on standby by Police following report of a male having fallen from High Force waterfall. Local Team members on scene along with rope rescue group, but full Team not deployed. Body recovered the following day by Police Underwater Unit.
2300 11/04/2007	Search Dog Skye & Handler responded to call out via SARDA to assist North Of Tyne & Northumberland National Parks Mountain Rescue Team for Missing Male from the Washington Town area (Tyne & Wear). Missing person found outside initial search area.
1815 25/03/2007	18.15 hrs request to assist Cleveland Search and Rescue Team in search for missing person on the North Yorks Moors. 14 Team members and two Team SARDA dogs attended. Missing person located by Team early in search.
2315 22/03/2007	23.25 hrs as Team were returning to Base following previous call-out, request by Police to search for a missing vulnerable male in the Darlington area. Open ground and urban search. Assisted by Police helicopter and one Team SARDA dog. Stood down at 03.00 hrs. Nothing found. Missing man identified as patient in hospital the following morning.
1630 22/03/2007	16.30 hrs request by Police to search for vulnerable male missing from nursing home in the Seaham area. Search open ground and urban areas, assisted by Police helicopter and 2 Team SARDA dogs. Stood down at 23.00 hrs when person found safe outside of search area.
0915 10/03/2007	09.15 hrs - brief Standby in relation to missing teenager in Durham. Turned up safe and well.
1700 15/02/2007	Team member gave immediate care to a person who collapsed whilst on a train journey
1930 10/02/2007	19.30 hrs request by Police to locate several drivers reporting as snowbound on a moorland road in NW Durham. Team members located 9 persons including an 8 week old baby, caught in drifting snow. Team SARDA dog Skye located two of the vehicles. Baby and mother evacuated by Team, before rest of vehicles dug out by road clearing equipment.
0800 10/02/2007	08.00 hrs two Team members en route to Team training came across a car and driver stuck in white out conditions. Assistance given and escorted off hills to clear roads.

1530
03/02/2007

15.30 hrs standby and consultation with Police in relation to a missing person. Team stood down after two hours following further information.

0315
31/01/2007

03.15 hrs request to assist Swaledale Mountain Rescue Team in search for missing vulnerable elderly male in Yorkshire Dales. Team search group and search dog Holly attended at first light. Missing person found by member of the public outside immediate search area.

1500
27/01/2007

55 Year old climber, whilst descending from the summit of Aconcague to Base camp slipped and fell off the ice bridge into a crevasse. Team member assisted to recover the uninjured climber before the situation worsened.

15.30
19/01/2007

15.30 hrs Team requested to assist in search for missing child. Stood down en route when child located safe.

1300
12/01/2007

52 Year old climber, after descending from the summit of Aconcagua became exhausted and hyperthermic whilst trying to recover outside of a tent at Base camp. Fluids, food and warmth administered until the climber was cared for by friends.

1300
05/01/2007

Team members recovered sheep from cragfast location on river Tees near Barnard Castle. Request from Fire Service.

0630
13/12/2006

06.30 hrs request by Police to assist in search for missing vulnerable 14 year old girl in the Chilton area of County Durham. Search of woodland by Team and two SARDA dogs proved negative. Assisted by Police helicopter. Girl later turned up safe well outside of search area.

2310
29/11/2006

Team members returning home from team training found a small van that had been driven off the road on to what the driver thought was solid ground but was in fact wet mud and had become stuck. The Team members used a Team members private 4x4 vehicle to drag the van back onto the road. The driver had been there some time before being rescued.

2230
29/11/2006

Team members returning home from training discovered abandoned car at side of road between watershed and Bollihope. Car had been spotted some hours earlier en-route to training. Inspection of the car revealed map of local area in back seat and approach shoes and socks in passenger foot well indicating someone had changed footwear. The Police informed. Approximately one mile down the road, two walkers were spotted in darkness by the Team members. When questioned revealed they were doing some navigation practice but had become a little waylaid and had forgotten to leave a note in their vehicle.

0415
26/11/2006

04.15 hrs request by Police to assist in search for elderly vulnerable male missing from Bishop Auckland General hospital. Search commencing when he was located safe and well. Police helicopter attended.

1730
20/11/2006

17.30 hrs consultation request from Police in respect of a vulnerable person missing from home. Subsequently traced to an area out of county and referred via Police and ourselves to the MRT in that area.

0630
07/11/2006

06.30 hrs request by Police to search for vulnerable elderly male missing from home in Catchgate area of Co Durham. Search of woodland and farmland. Assisted by Police helicopter and 3 SARDA dogs. Missing person found by Team at 15.15 hrs wandering in search area, he was unharmed having spent two days and nights out in the open.

1415
15/10/2006

14.15 hrs Durham Police recieved 999 call from a Duke of Edinburgh Award expedition group, who reported difficulties and one member suffering from hypothermia, in the Yorkshire dales area. Police contacted TWSRT Control on airwave and the Team Controller, on making mobile contact with the group, directed the Police helicopter, which was attending our ongoing search nearby, to the scene. Swaledale MRT then responded on the ground to this incident.

0830
15/10/2006

Search for male missing from his home in Co Durham, continued from 9th October. TWSRT provided control alongside Kirby Stephen MRT, Swale MRT and supported by Penrith MRT, Scarborough MRT, Cleveland SRT, Northumberland National Parks SRT and North of Tyne SRT. Over 70 searchers involved in a search of forest and open fell in Cumbria, supported by Durham Police and Police helicopter. Body of missing person located.

0400
14/10/2006

04.00 hrs call to assist NNPSRT and NOTSRT in search for teenage male lost and reported injured in Chopwell woods. Team SARDA dog Holly and two personnel sent in initial response - rest of Team on standby. Missing person located after 2 hours and prior to full Team deployment.

0800
09/10/2006   The Team were called to assist in a search by Kirby Stephen Mountain Rescue Team for a forty year old man whose car had been found near some woodland. The coniferous woodland was extremely dense and searching proved very slow. Two Team SARDA dogs attended. Swale MRT and Penrith MRT also attended along with the Police helicopter from the North East. Nothing found

1730
06/10/2006   Team Dog called to assist in search for missing elderly person following his car crashing into the river Swale. Passing Team member also assisted.

2032
13/09/2006   Team Member assisted young lady laying in the street semi conscious with blood from lacerations on her arms. County ambulance was called. Lady taken to Darlington Hospital.

1430
09/09/2006   14.30 hrs request by Police to assist in search for missing vulnerable child in Stanley area. Team and 3 SARDA dogs en route when stood down as girl turned up safe.

1630
25/08/2006   16.30 hrs - Information from Police - request for help recieved after a 4 year old black Labrador 'Sam' fell down a 35 foot deep mine shaft whilst out on a grouse shoot on Catterick Moss near Frosterley. 11 Team members attended and 'Sam' was safely recovered up the vertical shaft to the surface. 'Sam' was unhurt from his ordeal.

1720
24/08/2006   Received call from police at 17.20hrs to search for missing female on Cockfield Fell. Search of Fell by Team members, Police and Police Helicopter. Missing female found safe and well by Team Search Dog (Misty).

0730
13/08/2006   Callout following a request from Penrith MRT to assist in a major search in the Brampton area of Cumbria for a missing 75 year old and his dog. We joined Teams from the Lake District, Scotland, Dales, Northumberland and RAF Leeming in the search. Missing person found following day after dog alerted villages. Only minor injuries. Found outside search area

1815
11/08/2006   Vulnerable male adult missing from home for 8 hours in the Newton Aycliffe area. Initial search by SARDA dog and 2 team members. Male returned home.

1721
09/08/2006   The Team were called out to a man and child stuck above High Force Waterfall in Teesdale. The pair were safely rescued by the fire service as the Team assembled.

1956
01/08/2006   Team called to Lanehead Quarry, Stanhope to rescue an injured female whom had fallen down into the quarry and come to rest on a ledge. A police Helicopter rescued the injured female as the Team assembled.

1140
30/07/2006   Teesdale & Weardale Search & Rescue Team were called out to one of their more unusual rescues on Sunday afternoon. Three sheep had been reported by a dog walker stuck on a ledge 10mts up a quarry face in Bollihope Quarry, Frosterley, Weardale Co. Durham. The sheep had been on the ledge since at least Saturday morning. Durham & Darlington Fire & Rescue Service attended on Saturday evening and after consulting with the farmer and the RSPCA it was decided to leave the sheep overnight to see if they could get down themselves. The sheep were still on the ledge on Sunday morning so it was decided to call out the Search & Rescue Team later in the day to recover the sheep. Team Controller Adam Hearn said "When we arrived two of the sheep had disappeared, we can only assume they managed to get down safely themselves. Unfortunately a lamb did not have the same courage so we needed to recover it. Two team members were lowered to the ledge and after some difficulty managed to catch the lamb, secure it to a harness and then the rescuer and the lamb were lowered to the ground. After a quick check the lamb seemed none the worse for wear and wandered off. We even got a round of applause from the sizable crowd who had gathered to watch.

1930
24/07/2006   19.30hrs Call out by Police to search for missing female in Hamsterley Forest area. Police helicopter also involved in search. Missing woman found safe as Team assembled. Stood down.

1000
23/07/2006   Team present at Great North Walk near Darlington. Assistance given to 8 casualties.

1100
22/07/2006   A man was reported missing to Durham Police on Friday evening (21st July). The police were concerned for his safety following a phone message sent to one of his friends. They contacted Teesdale & Weardale Search & Rescue Team on Saturday morning who concentrated the search on Beamish Woods to the north east of Beamish Museum. Thirty members of three mountain rescue teams (North or Tyne Search and Rescue Team and Northumberland National parks Search and Rescue Team) spent six hours on Saturday afternoon (22nd July 2006) searching dense woodland for the 33 year old man who had gone missing from West Pelton near Chester-le-Street. Three SARDA dogs were also deployed. Following a six hour search where no trace of the young man was found the search was called off.

1400
12/07/2006   14.00 hrs standby to North Of Tyne Search and Rescue Team/Northumberland National Parks Search and Rescue Team in relation to search for missing male. Team stood down at 16.00 hrs - not required. Missing person located in hospital.

1230 15/05/2006	12.20 hrs Call out to assist Penrith MRT in search of High Pennine for lost male walker. Weather wet and cold. Team starting search of ground above Cow Green reservoir, along with two Team SARDA dogs, when missing walker located safe by RAF Sea King Helicopter at High Cup Nick. Kirby Stephen SMRT also attended.
1330 09/05/2006	Request by Police to search for missing 35 year old male near Peterlee. Search of a local Dene, comprising steep, wooded and difficult terrain. Two Team SARDA dogs also attended along with support from Police helicopter. Nothing found and search stood down at 21.30 hrs. Body of missing person found 4 days later
1400 23/04/2006	14.00 hrs Team on exercise when called by Police to assist at High Force waterfall following reports of a person with a broken leg. Ambulance and Air ambulance also attending. Team stood down en route as person evacuated by Ambulance.
1645 10/04/2006	A teenage girl went missing from her home in Newton Aycliffe at 19.00 on Sunday 9th April. The Team were called mid afternoon the following day and searched the open and scrub land surrounding and near the missing girls home. In addition to police dogs the Team deployed three SARDA dogs. Nothing was found - Team stood down to await further developments. Girl found safe outside search area the following day.
1330 09/04/2006	13.30 hrs Request by Police to attend Cow Green reservoir, following report of a male with arm injuries following a fall. Weather was cold with frequent snow showers. Incident had taken place on Cauldron Snout and the injured man was assisted by passing walkers. Team en route, along with ambulance and Air ambulance. Casualty evacuated by helicopter - assisted by Team member. Team stood down.
1250 02/04/2006	12.50 Call -out by Police to person taken ill at High Force waterfall. Initial on scene reports indicated need for mountain rescue assistance. Team stood down en route, when Air ambulance able to evacuate casualty.
2025 01/04/2006	20.25 hrs request by Police to search for a 59 year old male missing from home. Believed to be despondent. Mobile phone call traced to area of open ground near Shildon - search commencing when he was found on a road and taken to hospital. 1 Team SARDA dog also attended.
0700 25/03/2006	Search continued in Cumbria for missing 74 year old male. Team searched area around High Cup Nick. 17 other MRT's and 120 personnel involved, in addition to 3 RAF Sea Kings. Search controlled by Penrith MRT and Kirby Stephen SMRT. Nothing found

0500 23/03/2006	05.00 hrs Team called to Cumbria to assist in search for missing 74 year old male in area at foot of Pennine fells. Search lead by Kirby Stephen SMRT and Penrith MRT. Keswick MRT, Kendal MRT, Patterdale MRT, RAF Leeming MRT and Moffat MRT also attended along with SARDA Lakes and RAF Sea King. Search stood down at 15.30 hrs. Nothing found
1215 19/03/2006	The Team were on a training exercise when at 12.15 they were called to assist with the evacuation of a female walker. The walker had a suspected leg fracture and was in a wooded ravine near Westgate in Weardale. Stanhope fire crew also attended and the casualty was evacuated to a waiting Air Ambulance.
0215 14/03/2006	02.00 hrs Request by Police to assist in search for despondent male missing from home in Darlington - one Team SARDA dog and support group deployed in initial response. Missing person returned home safe as search about to start.
1830 10/03/2006	18.30 hrs Police request to search for 14 year old vulnerable girl missing since before dark, in Easington area. Search stood down at 20.30 hrs when she turned up safe well outside search area. 16 Team members attended along with 1 SARDA dog.
1530 03/03/2006	Search for missing female in the coastal area near Peterlee. Coastguard search teams and police helicopter also involved. Two SARDA dogs and search teams deployed. The weather was very cold. The search stood down after 4 hours with nothing found. Missing woman turned up safe outside of search area early the following morning.
2030 11/01/2006	Stand by for missing male in the Darlington area
1940 09/01/2006	Search for (another) missing elderly gentleman who had gone off on a daily walk of about 0.5 miles. Search developed as more sightings came in. Suspended in the small hours for continuation as NESRA shout the following morning. Missing person found wandering in Sedgefield as NESRA Teams start to assemble.
1430 09/01/2006	Search for elderly gentleman missing from home since previous day. Initial search started 30 minutes before night fall and principle corridors were searched. Search was to resume next morning but missing person was identified in hospital having been collected off the street in an unconscious state at 13.00.
1609 03/01/2006	A 37 year old woman had been missing for several days. The team were asked to look for her after she was seen by canoeists near the river Tees in Barnard Castle. The Team search dog and the police helicopter were deployed. The missing woman turned up at a friend's house shortly after the Teams search commenced.

0652
17/12/2005
A seriously damaged crashed car was found by the police on a rural road but no casualty had been found. Initial police searches for the 29 year old driver were negative. Police found missing man near his home shortly after the Team's search had commenced.

1002
22/11/2005
Team on standby to search marshy area near Kelloe following reports by member of the public of calls for help. Team stood down after about 20 minutes.

1350
02/11/2005
Vulnerable 15 year old boy missing since previous night. Requested by police to search area near to his home. Missing boy returned home of own accord as the Team assembled

1044
20/10/2005
Male had evaded the police in the Barnard Castle area as they tried to section him the previous night and had then disappeared. The Team started searching the most likely areas mainly around the river. The missing person turned up back at home shortly after searches commenced.

1530
15/10/2005
Multiple vehicle collision involving a minibus on the B6277 Mickleton road. 6 people treated by team Advanced Medic for minor injuries.

1945
08/10/2005
A family with two young children had got stuck in their 4x4 on a minor track and did not know their location. Pulling together all the information they could provide the Team Leader identified a probably location. This was confirmed when the vehicle was found by the police helicopter. A small group of Team Members went to the location in the Team's off road vehicle and assisted the family's vehicle back to the road.

2000
07/10/2005
Call from police to identify our suitability to assist with an urban rescue of two boys from a hole. Boys were rescued by alternative means before the Team was deployed.

2000
04/10/2005
The Team were called by the police for initial advice in respect of 60 year old male lost in Hamsterley forest. The Team leader consulted with Forest rangers and specific locations were identified. The Police helicopter located the missing person before the Team were deployed.

2100
27/09/2005
Police requested Team help in finding a 12 year old who had left school shortly after lunch. He had subsequently been seen on a cycle path. The boy was found by family members shortly after the Team deployed.

1245
17/09/2005
Requested by the police to assist with an incident where a male had fallen at High Force. The Team was called out because initial reports suggested difficult access. The casualty was evacuated as the Team arrived.

2313
09/09/2005   An 11 year old child was missing for several hours. Child found by police as Team assembled.

2330
06/09/2005   30 year old male mountain biker reported missing in Hamsterley forest. Missing person located by the police helicopter and escorted out of the forest by the Team vehicle.

0052
04/09/2005   Called by the Penrith Team to help in a search for two vulnerable walkers who had reported themselves lost by mobile phone. The missing walkers were found by a rescue helicopter shortly after the Team deployed.

1930
21/08/2005   Team called to Merrybent area of Darlington to search for missing from home 84 year old male. Search of farmland and woodland. The Team was supported by police helicopter and police dog section. The body of the missing person was located close to where he was last seen.

1733
13/08/2005   A couple out walking reported themselves lost in Hamsterley forest (using a mobile phone). One of the missing persons suffered from diabetes and had run out of food. A police helicopter managed to locate the missing couple. The helicopter evacuated the diabetic while the remainder of the party were evacuated using a Team Vehicle.

1410
06/08/2005   6 year old male sustained injury on left knee after being run over by a quad bike. 66 year old female also injured by the same quad bike. This casualty received minor leg injury, and advised to go to A & E if symptoms worsen.

2203
02/08/2005   A motorist was flagged down by some youths who said a friend was stuck on a nearby rock face. The Team quickly assembled but could find no sign of the youths or their car.

2040
30/07/2005   Search for missing middle aged male believed to be at significant risk of self harm. Team deployed at first light (30/07/05) to area near Richmond to assist in NESRA search that had been going on over night. The missing person was found by a SARDA dog and the Team assisted in the evacuation to County Ambulance.

1730
24/07/2005   Elderly female Alzheimer's sufferer reported missing from home. Found by police as Team assembled.

1400
24/07/2005   3 casualties treated and sent to Hospital while Mountain Biking at Hamsterley Forest.

1330
12/07/2005   Young male went missing following an 18th Birthday celebration. After initial search by his friends the police were called. Initial checks proved negative and the Team were called out. The missing person was quickly found safe and well and escorted back to the police by Team members.

1000
10/07/2005   14 participants of the Great North Walk assisted with a range of injuries - six of which were classified as serious.

1000
09/07/2005   Team on Standby to assist Swaledale Mountain Rescue Team during their search in the Richmond area.

2030
03/07/2005   Request by police to assist in search for two missing boys aged 9 and 10 in the Peterlee area. One of the boys was additionally vulnerable in respect of a medical condition. Boys found safe by police as Team assembled.

0930
23/06/2005   Continuation of previous search. Result was again negative. Missing person turned up safe the following day outside the scope of the search.

1745
22/06/2005   Search for missing 66 Year old male from Bishop Auckland, Eldon Lane area. Missing Person after his evening meal went for his evening walk which normally took about 60 Mins. Missing Person suffers from angina & a stroke from 2 years ago. Searched all local pathways and know walk routes. Nothing found

1455
22/06/2005   Call from Northumberland National Parks Search and Rescue Team following a call to them relaying request for help from a walker with a twisted knee and lost in mist on Cross Fell. Penrith Mountain Rescue Team alerted and TWSRT Team leader spoke to relatives - Team on standby to assist until Penrith Mountain Rescue Team located walker at 18.45 hrs safe.

2330
19/06/2005   Standby to assist in possible North East Search and Rescue response to flash flooding in North Yorkshire and reports of several people missing. Team on standby through night - not required.

1437
15/06/2005   Walker contacted TWSRT on his mobile phone and reported himself lost. Following further discussion with the missing walker some directions were given and a Team member was sent to Moorhouse where the missing walker was duly found.

1300
15/06/2005   Lamb and Ewe crag fast at Holwick Scars - both sheep fell before rope in place

2020
13/06/2005   Requested to search for a female in her 70's suffering from Alzheimer's. The missing lady had left her home about eight hours earlier to "walk to Rookhope". The Team's search found more sightings. The missing person approached a member of the public at about 22.20 who contacted the police. Team medics checked the missing person over and found her in good physical health.

1201
02/06/2005   Ewe and lamb cragfast at Holwick Scar for 2 days - recovered by team member using ropes

2130
30/05/2005   Call from Police in respect of a male missing from home in Darlington and possibility of his car being located in Dale during the night. Small response group on standby through night, involving advanced casualty career and SARDA dog. No further developments

0840
20/05/2005   Team members assisted with Cas Care treatment of female who had been involved in RTA. Female driver possible had spinal injuries. Casualty stabilized until County Ambulance arrived.

1830
19/05/2005   Called by police following find of male clothing neatly folded near river wear at Willington. Search of immediate area, and river banks supported by Team canoe group and SARDA dog Meg. Nothing found - river pools identified for Police to search with underwater unit.

1200
16/05/2005   Call by police to assist in search for male - in hills between Stanhope and Egglestone, possible self harm. Duty Controller advised of priority areas and person was located by Police helicopter, and evacuated to hospital as Team assembled.

1130
28/04/2005   Army Cadet undertaking his Duke of Edinburgh fell and injured his ribs. Assisted off the fells by team members.

1520
09/04/2005   Duke of Edinburgh group from assisted out of the Cauldron Snout area during bad weather. Group took shelter in the High Force Youth Hostel overnight and continued their expedition the following morning.

1201
26/03/2005   Requested by police to search for missing from home male, who was considered to be at risk. Police enquiries & searches suggested that he may have travelled to the Broken Scar area. A hasty search was carried out in the early evening using the last of the light. Nothing found. Missing male turned up at home later safe & well at a friend's house.

1222
26/03/2005   Standby to assist Swaledale Team

1100
22/03/2005   Call out by Crook police to assist in search around the St. Johns Chapel area for male who rang 999 stating he was going to harm himself. Mobile phone located to specific area. Air support not available due to poor visibility. Police off road bikes deployed. Initial search of area, negative. New information received and relocated search to Frosterley area. Police stood search down to make further enquiries.

0645
21/03/2005   Team member first on scene at serious RTA. 21 year old male struck by bus. Immediate care given, however the person died at the scene.

0430
14/03/2005   Requested by police to search for missing 15 Year old girl in Consett area -Weather cold. Search of woodland & open ground. 2 SARDA dogs assisted plus RAF Helicopter. Missing person returned home at 0800hrs.

1800
12/03/2005   Police receive 999 call from two male walkers lost - mobile phone trace identifies area at Scargill Moor near Bowes. Control and search group (6) respond to assist police fixed wing aircraft. Lost walkers located some distance away in Swaledale on Water Crag. Swaledale MRT & TWSRT located & located evacuate walkers - unharmed. Terrain difficult under foot, large areas of deep wet snow.

1636
07/03/2005   Requested by police to search Broken Scar for missing vulnerable female missing from home since 11.10hrs. Mobile phone signal indicated in the Broken Scar area. Canoe group responded to search river & river banks in the immediate area supported by India 88. Nothing found. Missing person later reported to be outside of the area.

1310
05/03/2005   Requested by police to assist in rescue of snowbound car with 3 passengers on Stanhope / Blanchland road. Police vehicle also snowbound. Land Rover & 10 team members attended, driving through white out conditions & deep drifting snow to reach police car. Team members walked through 4 feet deep snow to car & evacuated 3 people back to team Land Rover.

1741
03/03/2005

Call out from Fire Control & Police. Dog cragfast on 250 foot high quarry face since 3pm. Fire Crews unable to effect rescue. Team members attended, dog retrieved on 250 foot lower by 2 team members & re-united with owner - uninjured. Conditions, deep snow cover and dark. Para Flares used to illuminate scene.

0930
27/02/2005

Call by police - missing female from Tow Law - in car threatening suicide. Mobile "Pinged" location 5km radius of Tow Law. Indications accessing Fell. Has previously been subject to search before. 3 Team members search key focal points along with police. Missing person located in car. Taken to hospital.

2100
26/02/2005

17 Year old female left hospital stating that she was going for a coffee at the nearby Airport. Search commenced. Nothing found.

1230
24/02/2005

Team leader alerted to stranded driver on Cowshill / Allenheads road - following news report on radio Newcastle. 4 Foot snow drifts, driver had been there since 7am. Enquiries to NOTSRT, police establish no one aware of this. Radio station receives further info at 13:15hrs from driver. - Still stuck in car half buried. Position confirmed as County Border above Cowshill, Weardale. Team Leader spoke to driver (Whom was now getting concerned). NOTSRT link up with snow clearing machines from Northumberland - TWSRT on standby - Durham Police activate snow clearing machines from Weardale - Local Team Members liaises with crews at the scene. Driver recovered from car & snow, safe & well.

1330
24/02/2005

Call out request by police to 8 Month pregnant woman stranded on Castleside / Stanhope road in a Land Rover -White out conditions & severe drifting. Police vehicles snow bound 3 miles from scene. Air ambulance unable to fly - RAF Boulmer preparing to attempt an assist. Team members access scene in tractors & snow ploughs. Woman recovered by tractor to Stanhope. Police officers & BBC Film Crew evacuated back to A68.

1530
24/02/2005

Call Out request by police, report of distressed driver stuck on A68. Severe snow drifting. Team Land Rover & crew search road from Castleside to Tow Law. Nothing found. All incidents receive extensive TV & Radio coverage, including live BBC radio link as incidents progressed. Events covered on National TV news.

1201
31/01/2005

Review with Police. Search continued. 2 team members re-visited specific areas in daylight & canoe search group prepared for river search. Missing person found by member of public safe & well in main shopping area, having slept rough in woodland overnight.

1945
30/01/2005

Requested by police to search for missing 54 year old male - vulnerable. Search of woods & open ground including urban parks & cemeteries in Barnard Castle. Assisted by India 99. SARDA dog also deployed. Searched until 01.00hrs on 31/01/05 - nothing found.

1245
16/01/2005

Team called by police following report of elderly male entering river Wear at Hunwick near Bishop Auckland. Team training with RAF Sea King at the time. 7 Team members flown direct to scene - Police helicopter & Fire Service also in attendance. Team member in RAF Sea King commenced search whilst Team members on ground prepared search alongside Fire personnel. Body located downstream and winched to riverbank by RAF Helicopter.

0937
12/01/2005

39 Year old male MFH. Search established nothing found. MHF returned home 2 days later safe & well.

1400
31/12/2004

Requested by police to search for MFH. Search of Pennine Way / Bowlees Area. Missing person located by Team Member en-route to Bowlees.

0830
03/12/2004

Team member arrived at an RTA after police but before ambulance. Carried out primary survey and applied cervical collar to female driver before handing over to County Ambulance.

13.00
24/11/2004

Search of River Tees from Winston Bridge to Gainford by Canoe Team for "Distressed mid 20s Female". Nothing found.

1930
23/11/2004

Barnard Castle police received report from passing driver of mid 20s female looking in a very distressed state standing on Winston Bridge over the Tees river. The car driver turned his car round the female was nowhere to be seen. No persons reported missing by police. Nothing found.

1100
21/11/2004

Called by Police to assist a Canoeist pinned in the water. Canoeist was unconscious. Upon arrival the female Canoeist was on shore and Police, Fire Brigade & Air Ambulance had arrived. Casualty kept in Hospital overnight suffering from fluid inhalation.

2251
11/11/2004

Search for 83 year old male suffering from Alzheimer's by diabetic missing from Care home. Last seen at 1500hrs. Called out at 2251hrs. Body of missing person found at 0126hrs.

1730
07/11/2004   Search for elderly woman seen in distress in the area around Killhope - Upper Weardale. Open moorland - Weather cold & wet. Search about to commence when she was located in a nearby village safe & well.

2015
06/11/2004   Request by Penrith MRT to assist in search for male walker, benighted & distressed on the Pennine Way in the High Cup Nick area. Weather -wet & poor visibility. Person found with hypothermia by Penrith MRT team member 2 hours into search.

1900
13/10/2004   Team member assisted male knocked down on crossing by car. Head Injuries

1640
09/10/2004   76 Year Old Male missing from nursing home in Tow Law. Found by neighbour in Crook as search commenced.

0050
29/09/2004   7 Year old boy had gone missing at 21:30 hrs to look for his bike. All friends & family connection enquiries were negative & at 00:50hrs the concern was at such a level that a full scale search & response was established. Police following up a reported sighting of him that evening with a male; was found at an address in Shildon.

1600
25/09/2004   Search for 50 year old Pennine Way walker who had become lost around the Maize Beck area due to following guide book and not the OS Map. Walker located by Helicopter following direction from Teesdale Base.

2350
13/09/2004   Standby - Request to assist Police in search for missing 80 Year Old Alzheimer's male. Found safe & well by Police before Team deployed.

1400
12/09/2004   2 team members covering the LDWA 15, 28 & 50 walks assisted with Cas Care treatment to a competitor who had sprained his ankle.

2115
12/09/2004   2 team members covering the LDWA 15, 28 & 50 walks assisted 3 competitors who had become lost on their route. Team members assisted the competitor for 4 hours until the next check-point.

1230
11/09/2004   2 team members covering the LDWA 15, 28 & 50 walks assisted with Cas Care treatment to a Jean wearing competitor on the 50 mile walk who had twisted his ankle.

1200	
03/09/2004	Standby - Possible search for missing person following the discovery of abandoned car at Derwentside Reservoir. Missing person located safe & well by Police before Team deployed.

1100	
02/09/2004	Standby - Possible search for missing female missing in the Finchale Priory area. Missing person located by Police before team deployed.

1215	
30/08/2004	Search for possible victim of assault. A woman had been found heavily bloodstained & claimed to have hurt someone. Search of woodland & Farmland. Helicopter assists. Nothing found. Police enquiries continue

1600	
29/08/2004	"US Jeweller stuck 250 yards down mine" Male explorer was pinned down after a rock fall. Fire Brigade personnel had recovered injured male to the entrance of the mine. Injured male was transported to local hospital by Sea King

2100	
27/08/2004	Report of woman being swept away in a dinghy on the River Tees. Team alerted as soon as Police received call. Local team member arrived at scene with Police. Woman had returned safely, having apparently being swept upto 1km and then scrambled up steep river banks.

0000	
20/08/2004	Call to search after RTA. Driver of vehicle missing from the scene, feared injured. Driver located and examined by Team medics.

0830	
15/08/2004	M/F/H 65 Year Old Female, last seen at 2000hrs on the 14/08/04. Missing person turned up safe & well on scene at 10.19hrs.

0630	
12/08/2004	78 Year Old M.F.H. Alzheimer's missing since 0730hrs on 10/08/04. M.F.H turned up at 1400 hrs on 12/08/04.

1530	
21/06/2004	15 year old male, missing from secure unit, North of Tyne called for assistance. Missing person located by police at 1810

1400	
20/06/2004	Request by police to search for 15 Year old male, Missing from home. Causey Arch area thoroughly searched before team were stood down. Person found safe & well by police / Family.

1830
18/06/2004   Search for missing walker who had not returned to his tent. Missing 55 year old male found by team members.

1415
30/05/2004   Witness to an RTA, 2 Vehicles, 13 Year old Female, and Facial Injuries.

1100
15/05/2004   60 Year old Male, Possible hip injury, Casualty Care treatment offered.

0930
03/05/2004   50 Year Old Male M.F.H , search of all neighbouring woodland, Body found by Police Air Support at1505hrs

0000
01/05/2004   46 Year old male, M.F.H, Team put on stand by. Missing person returned home " 0330hrs

0900
18/04/2004   Search continues for male missing from home since 25/3. . Search of dense undergrowth. Nothing found.

0900
10/04/2004   Clothing found near tarn on Cronkley Fell. The clothing was weighted down with stones. Nothing found.

1410
10/04/2004   Dog had fallen down the south side of the River near High Force. Dog recovered by Team members after being moved by member of public. Dog transported to Vets at 15.10hrs

1000
03/04/2004   39 Year Old male left home at 2pm saying that he was going for a walk, Unusual behaviour, took outdoor clothes & rucksack. His personal mobile phone was switched off. Body located in stream near bridge.

1115
24/03/2004   36 Year old male missing from home. Body found by Police in near by woodland.

1430
07/03/2004   Teddy bear & note found attached to bench at broken scar. Large scale search involving Police Air Support, Police & TWSRT. Nothing Found.

1225
17/02/2004   34 year old male, Went missing from Farm where car had been left. Missing person found safe & well

1425
05/02/2004   Dog trapped down cave / fissure in rock. Rescue attempts unsuccessful. Cave / fissure backfilled as no signs of life from the dog.

1432
09/01/2004   47 year old vulnerable male missing in the Barnard Castle Area, Missing person located out of area.

1845
06/01/2004   Team on standby for missing male, stood down en-route. Missing person found safe & well.

1201
03/01/2004   Team put on standby for possible search for missing male in Wensleydale, Team stood down.

1350
31/12/2003   Request by Police to search for MFH. Search of Pennine Way/ Bowlees area. Missing person located by team member en-route to Bowlees. safe & well

1201
15/11/2003   Team put on standby for search for missing female. Located safe by police outside of area.

1430
05/11/2003   Request by Police to search for missing from home vulnerable 30 year old male. Search of farmland assisted by Police aircraft. Found safe out of search area, having travelled to scene of childhood holidays.

1300
05/11/2003   Team on short standby to respond to incident in Swaledale. Not required – Air Ambulance attended.

1140
12/10/2003   Cas Care treatment given to Fell runner who became de-hydrated

0900
09/10/2003   Request by Police to search for 82 year old male missing from home. Search of River Tees, using Team canoe section. Body found and recovered.

0700
08/10/2003   Search continues at first light, extending to open fell. Assisted by police helicopter and Kirkby Stephen MRT. Nothing found. Missing person turned up safe at home 30 miles away the following day.

2200
07/10/2003   Request to search for driver missing from RTA. Believed injured. Search of woodland / roads. Nothing found

2220
01/10/2003   Request by Police to search for missing 50 year old vulnerable male. SARDA dog
standby and Police aircraft assisted. Search of urban area found under bushes by Team,
mildly hypothermic. Evacuated to County Ambulance. Weather very cold.

0900
14/09/2003   Search continues for missing male in Ferryhill. Nothing found. Turned up back at home 3
months later. Had been living in hostels.

1215
27/08/2003   Request by RSPCA to extricate a cow in calf which had fallen over a 60 foot cliff into a
ravine. Other agencies unable to assist after assessment. Team member and Team vet,
visited site and advised evacuation attempt would be too traumatic for the cow, and
would further complicate injuries sustained. Farmer advised to have the cow put down.

0900
23/08/2003   Request by Police to search for missing from home 54 year old male -last seen 12 days
earlier. Search of woodland and disused quarries. Nothing found. MFH Turned up at
home address 4 days later very confused.

1130
17/08/2003   Police request Team members present at Police Public event to assist 53 year old female
motorcyclist who had fallen from her machine at low speed. Foot injury. Transported in
Team Control vehicle to Hospital.

1000
30/07/2003   Request by Cleveland Police and Cleveland SRT to search disused quarry in respect of
a missing male despondent from their area. CSRT assisted. Search of quarry face, cave
entrances on face and wooded areas. Nothing found. Teams stood down when missing
person located by Police in hospital.

0755
21/07/2003   Request by Police to search for persons, believed vulnerable following discovery of van
parked overnight with note left. Search of surrounding area and River Tees. Missing
couple turned up safe as search progressed. Police helicopter involved in initial search.

0845
21/07/2003   Two team members responding to above call-out came upon a serious RTA, involving a
burning car and three casualties. Immediate care given prior to arrival of road and Air
Ambulance. 1 fatality. Police counselling offered.

1400
16/07/2003   Standby by police for search for missing vulnerable male. Found following call from
members of public, before Team mobilised.

1000
13/07/2003   Team members present at Great North Walk. 4,000 entrants in hot and sunny weather. 11 incidents dealt with, heat exhaustion, sprained ankles and angina complaints. 6 people evacuated off the fells by team. One casualty airlifted by Air Ambulance.

04/07/2003   Rescue of lamb from sink hole

1300
22/06/2003   Woman walker failed to reach checkpoint in organised walk. Initial search by Team members present negative. Woman had turned round and returned to start.

1300
08/06/2003   Request by Fire and Rescue Service to assist in rescue of Labrador dog cragfast 30m down a 150 foot cliff. Team crag group retrieved dog safely and returned to owner.

1300
11/05/2003   Team on standby, Fell incident in Swaledale, Air Ambulance evacuation. Team not required.

1430
11/05/2003   Search for 30 year old venerable male. Search of Farmland. Found 60 miles away in childhood haunt of Scarborough.

1201
03/05/2003   Cragfast sheep & dead lamb, rescued with rope.

1030
01/05/2003   Search for missing mother who abandoned car in Pittington. Assisted by CSRT, mounted Police, 1 SARDA & India 88. Search of farmland. Body found by CSRT in woodland 1.5km from car.

1201
19/04/2003   Team member assisted 50 year lady with sprained ankle. Evacuated to YHA.

1201
07/04/2003   Rescue of lamb from sink hole.

0930
30/03/2003   Request by NNPSRT to assist in search from missing vulnerable 82 year male. Found safe, as TWSRT Team members arrived.

1250
14/03/2003   Request by Police to search for missing despondent 17 year old male. Search of farmland and steep sided woodland. Missing person returned home safely as search progressed.

1201
08/03/2003   Team member assisted Air Ambulance in evacuation of lady who suffered head and arm injuries in fall.

1201
05/03/2003   Team member rescued cragfast sheep.

1045
28/01/2003   Request by Police to search for missing 40 year old despondent male. Search of steep sided woodland and coastal fringe. Supported by Cleveland SRT and two SARDA dogs. Police aircraft attended along with Coastguard search of inshore. Nothing found. Later turned up safe.

1100
28/01/2003   Team member assists at RTA - Student knocked off bike by car.

1200
26/01/2003   Search continues for missing 19 year old male. Search of woodland. Nothing found. Body later found by member of public 1KM from home in a hawthorn covered ditch beside road to Shotley Bridge.

2220
10/01/2003   Requested by police to search for missing vulnerable male, diabetic. Search of urban Barnard Castle & fringe woodland & river banks. Assistance from police air support. Found by team member under bushes. Evacuated to base - warmed up and diabetic state. Monitored until arrival of ambulance.

1030
05/01/2003   Request by Police to search for missing 35 year old mother, whose car was found abandoned in village. Assisted by Cleveland SRT, 1 SARDA dog, Cleveland Mounted Police and Police Aircraft. Search of farmland, disused quarries and woodland. Body found in woodland 1.4km from village. No suspicious circumstances.

0800
05/01/2003   Request to assist Swaledale FRO and CSRT in search for missing 74 year old woman. Search of farmland. Footprints located entering frozen pond. Body later recovered by Police underwater unit.

1400
23/12/2002   Request by Police to assist in recovery of body, from difficult ground beneath Causey Arch. Fire and Rescue Service also attended and effected recovery as Team arrived.

1500
22/12/2002   Animal rescue. Local Team member out training dog, finds and releases sheep trapped under tree and entangled by wire. Assisted by other local Team members.

0820
16/12/2002   Team members assist at RTA. Teenage girl knocked down by car.

0900
08/12/2002   Search for missing 19 year old male continues. Search of river and woodland. Assisted
                   by 32 Police officers. Nothing found.

1201
05/12/2002   Team member assisted Ambulance crew at scene of serious RTA. Two fatalities and two
                   seriously injured.

2000
22/11/2002   Standby for search for missing male Alzheimer's sufferer. Team stood down before
                   search commenced – found safe in Durham.

1530
15/11/2002   NESRA call out standby for missing woman in Swaledale. Found before Team deployed.

1200
10/11/2002   Search continues for 19 year old male. Search of woodlands & open Ground.
                   Nothing Found.

1000
09/11/2002   Search continues. Team SARDA dog deployed to woodland areas. Nothing found

0900
29/10/2002   Search for missing 19 year old male continues. Additional Teams from NESRA assist in
                   widening search area to extensive woodland areas. Police helicopter assists. 46
                   personnel in attendance from TWSRT, Cleveland SRT, North of Tyne SRT, and Swaledale
                   Fell Rescue Organisation.

0900
27/10/2002   Search continues for missing from home 19 year old male. Team SARDA dog and Police
                   helicopter assist. Widened search of areas known to be visited by missing person.

1830
27/10/2002   Consultation request by Barnard castle Police, in respect of sighting of overturned canoe
                   in swollen River Tees. Police enquiries continued. Later discussion concluded canoe was
                   'lost' and not reported by owner. No further action required.

1700
26/10/2002   Request by Police to search for missing form home 19 year old despondent male.
                   Search of woodland and open ground close to his home. Assisted by Police helicopter.

1400
06/10/2002   Team member assisted cragfast youth to safety

2000
25/09/2002   Request by Police to search for 9 year old girl missing from home. Search commencing when girl located safe and well in nearby village.

1300
21/09/2002   Team members assist injured walker on steep ground. Evacuation by Glencoe MRT

1515
26/08/2002   Request by Police to search for missing 74 year old male Alzheimer's sufferer, separated from family on visit to Egglestone Hall. Police aircraft assisted search. Found, 5 hours later as darkness fell, almost 1 km away in open farmland. Safe and well.

1100
08/08/2002   NESRA standby for weekend search. Missing male. Stood down before Team deployed.

1600
04/08/2002   Request by Police to search for missing vulnerable 70 years old male. Car abandoned at start of regular short walk. Search of woods and parkland. SARDA dog deployed. Police fixed wing aircraft also involved. Nothing found. Missing person later found safe in Stanhope 25 miles away on morning of 5/8/02.

1400
03/08/2002   Request by Police to search for missing vulnerable 53 year old male. Search of open ground bordering urban area. Missing person located out of search area and taken to hospital by County Ambulance.

1845
22/07/2002   Call to assist mountain biker who had fallen and sustained suspected head and arm injuries. 1 mile stretcher evacuation to Team Land Rover and transfer to County Ambulance.

2000
21/07/2002   Request by Police to search for missing despondent male, traced by cell phone calls to the area. Police fixed wing aircraft assisted and located abandoned vehicle and later, the missing person 3 km away on open fell. Team evacuated to county ambulance.

1430
21/07/2002   Request by Police to search River Tees, following discovery of clothes, camping and fishing equipment on banks. Search located dinghy nearby. Nothing else found. Police enquiries continuing.

900
14/07/2002   Search continues for male missing from home. Search of woodland. Nothing found

1000
13/07/2002

Search continues for male missing from home since 25/3. Team assisted specialist search dog from South Yorkshire Police. Search of dense undergrowth. Nothing found.

1400
03/07/2002

Team asked to search for missing 53 year old. Search of woodland. Missing person located safe & well and taken to local Hospital for check-up.

1153
16/06/2002

Team on exercise, team member witnessed 14 year old boy who was participating in a large organised expedition training day, attempt to re-fuel a Trangia stove whilst still alight. Suffered burns to side of face and shock. Immediate care given and evacuated to group Supervisors. Advised to attend Hospital.

1200
10/06/2002

Team member assists cragfast youth on the Coast line at South Shields.

0900
09/06/2002

Request by Police to search 3 farms belonging to a farmer missing since 10th May. The farmer had been last seen 30 miles away and may have returned to farms. Missing person also believed to be despondent. Search of woodland and farmland.
Nothing found.

1430
02/06/2002

Team shadowing 'Roof of England Walks'. Female 78 years old separated from party near Cauldron Snout. Team searched Pennine way to intended destination of Widdybank Farm – negative. Search ready to escalate when missing person turned up safe and well at Langdon Beck YHA having left Pennine Way at Cauldron Snout and crossed Widdybank Fell.

1130
25/05/2002

Request to assist Penrith Mountain Rescue Team in search for missing 41 year old male walking from Dufton to Alston. Kirby Stephen SMRT, Kendal MRT and SARDA Lakes also attended. Last seen 24/5. Weather cool windy with heavy overnight rain. Becks in spate. TWSRT searched from Yad Moss. Penrith Team found man dead on summit of Green Fell on Pennine Way. He had not sought shelter, believed to have succumbed quickly. Stretchered off by PMRT.

1030
21/05/2002

Search for missing person. Subsequently found safe and well by Police in Peterlee on evening of 22/5/02.

1830
20/05/2002

Search for missing 71 year old Pennine Way walker. Separated from walking partner near Baldersdale. Search involved 1st phase; TWSRT assisted by police air support and RAF Sea king and SARDA dog. 2nd phase commenced 04.00 hrs involving additional 90 personnel from NNPSRT, NOTSRT, SFRO, CSRT, SDSRT, PMRT, KSSMRT, SARDA

LAKES – 3, SARDA ENGLAND –3, AND RAF LEEMING MRT. Air support from India 88 and RAF Sea king. Missing person located in Middleton at 10.30 hrs 21/5/02, having spent night in B and B and failed to notify walking partner or family. Extensive national media coverage.

2300
20/05/2002   Request by Police to assist in locating anonymously 999 reported RTA. Police air support unable to work due to poor weather. TWSRT Mobile despatched. Police located crashed vehicle.

1600
06/05/2002   Search for missing from home 62 years old despondent woman. Search of Tees around Broken Scar and search of urban area around South Park, River Skerne and adjacent woodland. Woman found alive, by Police, following reported sighting by security guards – in derelict house close to her home.

1145
26/04/2002   Search missing 69 year old vulnerable male. Assisted by Police Air support and Team SARDA dog. Nothing found. Team stood down 09.00hrs 27/4/02 man located in Hospital in Teesside.

1800
24/04/2002   Search continues for missing male. Total 500 Team hours to date. Nothing found. Search stood down until further evidence is received.

0900
21/04/2002   Search continues for missing male. Further river and land sectors covered. Nothing found

0900
06/04/2002   Search resumes for Mr Donnelly. Land and canoe river search. Nothing found.

0900
04/04/2002   Search for missing 53 year old male Eddie Donnelly. Despondent. Assisted by two members of North of Tyne Search and Rescue Team, Police Air support and Transport Police. Nothing found.

1100
29/03/2002   Stand by possible search for missing 15 year old boy from Northumbria Police Area (NOTSRT) last seen at Riverside Park. Team not required.

1201
16/01/2002   Body of elderly male found by Team SARDA dog handler following more information from Police.

1210
12/01/2002   Trainee Team member assists injured canoeist on River Tees.

2325
10/01/2002   Search for missing 59 Year old female, Dementia sufferer. NESRA stand by 03.00 hrs.
                  Team find lady trapped in locked school grounds. Hypothermic and foot injury. Evacuated
                  to Hospital.

2255
24/12/2001   Call out to search for despondent 39 year old woman. Team member enquires located
                  woman and Police make find overdosed taken to hospital. Team stood down en route

0830
16/12/2001   Search continues for missing male pensioner. Team searched steep ground alongside
                  reservoir and canoe search of reservoirs. Nothing found.

1300
06/12/2001   Call to assist Northumberland National Parks Search and Rescue Team in search for
                  vulnerable 80 year old missing from Sunniside since 04.00 hrs. Found in Causey wood
                  having fallen down steep bank and crossed river. Hypothermic - evacuated by Air
                  Ambulance to hospital

2359
02/12/2001   Request by Police to search open and wooded ground adjacent to Housing estate.
                  Missing 35 year old male, possible despondent. Assisted by police air support and Team
                  search dog. Finished 04.00 hrs. Nothing found. Team departs to resume search in
                  Lunedale. This search handed over to Northumberland National Parks Search and
                  Rescue Team and North of Tyne Search and Rescue Team at 09.00 hrs 2/12/01.
                  Nothing found – missing person turns up in Scotland safe.

0600
02/12/2001   Search resumes for Missing male. Assisted by Swaledale FRO and DEFRA Foot and
                  Mouth de-contamination unit. Nothing found.

1000
30/11/2001   Search continues for elderly missing male. Edge of Selset and forest edges searched.
                  Nothing found

0300
27/11/2001   Search for missing 78 year old Mr English. Car had been found abandoned edge of
                  Brownberry plantation. Assisted by police air support and Team Search dog.
                  Nothing found.

0830
19/11/2001   Evidence search requested by Police in the Stang Forest

1900
25/09/2001   Team alerted to possible request for assistance for canoeist who was seen in river.
                  Canoeist was brought safely to riverbank by his companions. Team stood down by police
                  after a few minutes.

1900
25/09/2001   Team alerted to possible request for assistance - Canoeist had capsized near Middleton
               Bridge - recovered, uninjured by colleagues.

1100
28/08/2001   Team asked by police to search for possible missing person following discovery of
               discarded tablet packets. Nothing found.

1100
28/08/2001   Team asked by police to search for possible missing person, following the discovery of
               a large quantity of discarded paracetamol wrappers in Flatts Wood. No trace of casualty.
               However team found approx £13,000 worth of cannabis plants being covertly cultivated
               in the wood.

0700
03/08/2001   Team asked by police to search for young man missing from home since early hours of
               Monday 30//2001. Wooded and steep ground searched. Body discovered by Team
               member.

0830
13/07/2001   Team asked by Police to search for vulnerable elderly man missing from home overnight.
               Turned up safe and well some miles away in Durham City.

1800
24/06/2001   Team member assisted at site of motorcycle RTA. 3 injured persons. One was airlifted to
               Hexham General Hospital by Air Ambulance.

2030
31/05/2001   Team asked by police to search for lady missing from home since 27/5/2001. Search
               continued on 1/6/2001. Nothing found. Body found some miles away several
               weeks later.

07/04/2001   Team members were returning to Base in a Team vehicle when they came across an
               RTA. They assisted casualty who was trapped in car until arrival of fire brigade.

04/04/2001   Team asked by police to search for man missing from home. Found safe and reasonably
               well. Taken to hospital by County Ambulance.

17/03/2001   Team asked by police to search River Wear with canoe group, for man missing from
               home for several weeks. Body found in river.
22/02/2001   Team asked by Swale Fell Rescue Organisation to assist in search for elderly man
               missing from home. Body found in River Swale

27/01/2001   Search continues from previous day. Nothing found. Body found in canal some
               weeks later.

26/01/2001	Team asked by Swaledale Fell Rescue Organisation to assist in search for man missing from home. Nothing found
07/01/2001	Team member assisted Swaledale Fell Rescue Organisation by arranging for search dogs to attend incident following the discovery of an unattended car
01/01/2001	Team members assisted county ambulance crew with evacuation of an elderly lady who had slipped and fallen and suffered fracture of the lower leg (it had snowed overnight).
01/01/2001	Team members discovered an elderly man lying in a stream at the bottom of an embankment (it had been snowing heavily and the casualty was intoxicated). Taken to hospital by county ambulance.
28/12/2000	Team member assisted elderly man who had collapsed while returning home from shopping. Taken to hospital by county ambulance.
0100 09/12/2000	As the previous search was finishing the police requested the Team to search for a second man missing from home. Nothing found. He turned up safe and well later that day.
1825 08/12/2000	Team called by police to search for patient missing from Hospital. Found suffering from Hypothermia on 9/12/2000
30/09/2000	Team called to assist Keswick MRT in search for elderly man missing from lodgings. Nothing found,
18/09/2000	Team called to search for missing walkers. Found safe and reasonably well, but flown to hospital by RAF helicopter.
12/09/2000	Team called by Police to search for young man missing from home. Tragically he was found dead, having, apparently, taking his own life near Esh Winning
22/08/2000	Team called to rescue dog which had fallen into disused mineshaft. Recovered uninjured. The only damage that occurred was to the training officer's hand.
19/08/2000	Team called by Police to search for elderly man missing from home. Missing person was an Alzheimer's sufferer. Nothing found. Still missing on 16 Sept. Assisted by Cleveland SRT.
29/07/2000	Team called by Police to recover three sheep which were stuck on a very steep riverbank. Farmer had already attempted single handed rescue, but had frightened himself when he realised how dangerous the situation was.
08/07/2000	Team called by Cleveland SRT to assist in search for missing hospital patient. Found safe and reasonably well some three miles from the area.

04/06/2000	Team called by Police to assist residents in South Church following severe flooding after the Gaunless burst its banks.
27/05/2000	Team called by Police to assist walker who had collapsed having suffered possible heart attack. Casualty was flown to hospital by RAF Sea King where unfortunately he was pronounced dead. Cauldron Snout
21/05/2000	Team members gave first aid to participant in Coast to Coast Cycle Ride who had fallen and suffered lacerations and grazes - between Consett and Beamish
21/05/2000	Team members rescued sheep which had fallen down disused mineshaft, after it was heard making a noise.
21/05/2000	Team called to assist County Ambulance crew with evacuation of man who had supposedly fallen near the old viaduct in Flatts Wood. Walked out to ambulance and was taken to hospital.
20/05/2000	Team members assisted cyclist who was injured when he was knocked from his bike during the Coast - to - coast cycle ride.
20/05/2000	Team called by Police to recover sheep which had fallen down a disused mine shaft. Unable to effect recovery due to fading light and lack of man power.
06/05/2000	Team members assisted Patterdale MRT with search for climber who had collapsed suffering from food poisoning Dovedale Lake District.
25/03/2000	Team called by Police to search for 13 year old boy who had been missing from home overnight. Found safe and well.
18/03/2000	Team called to assist County Ambulance crew with the evacuation of a lady with a fractured ankle just upstream of High Force Waterfall
14/01/2000	Team called by police to search for lady who had gone missing from home following a domestic dispute. Turned up safe and reasonably well some four miles away just as the search was about to begin.
0900 19/12/1999	Team members carried out further searches of river banks for man missing from home in Crook. This was a final effort. Nothing found. Mans body was found in the River Wear near Finchale Abbey on Monday 03/01/00 - subsequently identified as the man from Crook.
1000 18/12/1999	Team members carried out riverbank search for man missing from home in Crook
1615 14/12/1999	Small scale search following possible sighting of hand in river. Nothing found.

1000
13/12/1999 Team called by Police to search for man missing from home in Fir Tree. Found by search dog Meg.

1000
12/12/1999 Team members carried out further searches along old railway lines for man missing from home in Crook. See 09.12.1999

1000
11/12/1999 Team members+ search dog (Meg) carried out search for man missing from home in Crook SEE 273

0830
10/12/1999 Team carried out further search for man missing from home in Crook SEE 273

1815
09/12/1999 Team called by police to search for man missing from home in Crook. Nothing Found

1030
16/11/1999 Team member rescued 2 cragfast sheep - Fairy Dell Holwick

1550
14/11/1999 Team member assisted county ambulance crew with evacuation of a lady who had suffered a broken ankle near High Force Waterfall.

0930
08/01/1996 Team assisted Cleveland SRT in search for man missing from home. Body found by TWSRT team member

0700
15/10/1995 Team asked to search for man whose car had been found unattended. Had been missing overnight. Found in remote location by fell runner. Man had leg injury & hyperthermia. Evacuated by Air Ambulance

1745
11/10/1995 Twelve year old boy stumbled & suffered hip injury. Team member assisted until ambulance arrived.

24/09/1995 Mountain biker fell on steep downhill section & injured right hand side.

16/09/1995 Team on standby for possible search in the Eggleston area. Old lady turned up safe & well at home.

12/09/1995 Team asked to search for lady missing on the Pennine way. Turned up safe & well at home.

1415hrs 03/11/1994	Requested by police to search river and banks around broken scar / River Tees after discovery of teddy bear with note, indicating someone in distress. Search of river & area nothing found. Canoe group in attendance. Police aircraft & underwater unit in attendance.
21/08/1994	Team called by police to search for missing mountain biker in the Stang Forest. Lady turned up safe and well some distance away.
13/08/1994	Team called by police to search for man who had been swept over High Force waterfall. Body recovered by police underwater search unit.
10/07/1994	Team called by police to recover man suffering from spinal injury from shaft on Cockfield Fell.
0955 26/02/1994	Team member assisted elderly lady who had collapsed whilst waiting for a bus.
1900 03/02/1994	Team called by police to search an area south west of the Stang Forest for a man who had gone missing whilst walking on open fell during blizzard
2300 22/01/1994	Team asked to assist in search for man who had gone missing during the afternoon. Concern for his safety as he suffered from Alzheimer's. Stood down at 2330 when man was found safe & well.
1430 04/07/1993	Mountain Bike accident on Forest Track. Casualty treated by Red Cross personnel. Transported to Bedburn Car Park by Team Ambulance & taken to Bishop Auckland hospital by County Ambulance.
1300 04/07/1993	Mountain Bike accident on Forest track just outside the forest boundary. Casualty leg splinted by Red Cross Personnel - given entonox by team members. Transported to Forest track by team ambulance & taken to Bishop Auckland hospital by County Ambulance.
1545 28/06/1993	Boy knocked down by car. Team member administered first aid to casualty & reassured parents until arrival of County Ambulance.
1400 27/06/1993	Casualty was climbing on Brown Slabs when he fell (he was roped on) Team member who was climbing nearby, abseiled to casualty & lowered himself & casualty to base of crag. First aid treatment given for dislocated shoulder. Taken to hospital by companion.

1600
27/06/1993   Lady visitor to Hamsterley Forest felt unwell. Reassurance given. Hot Day, possibly resulted in the lady's illness. Taken to Bishop Auckland Hospital by County Ambulance.

1630
27/06/1993   Casualty fell from Mountain Bike & suffered abrasions to nose & arms. No other injuries. Wounds cleaned by team member.

1650
27/06/1993   Casualty was taking part in Durham Dales Challenge when he collapsed approx 300 meters after the checkpoint. Casualty taken to Bishop Auckland Hospital

03/01/1993   Casualty was in group walking down from High Raise to Wythburn in the Lake District when he stumbled and suffered fractured ankle. Team member in part raised the alarm on Mountain Rescue radio and injured walker stretchered off by Keswick Mountain Rescue Team.

24/12/1992   Sheep cragfast on Cronkley Scar. Recovered uninjured by Team member.

23/12/1992   Search for missing elderly lady near Barnard Castle. Body found by member of public on golf course.

13/12/1992   Search for man who had been missing in Cow Green area. Casualty found in hypothermic condition. Taken to hospital by County Ambulance. AS RECORD 362

04/11/1992   Team at Wheatsheaf, Staindrop for indoor training where asked to assist elderly man who had become unwell. Transferred to hospital by county ambulance.

16/10/1992   Man was grouse beating when he collapsed complaining of chest pains. Team member assisted until removal to hospital

27/09/1992   Boy fell off mountain bike in Hamsterley forest and suffered suspected fracture of collar bone. Taken to Bishop Auckland hospital in Red Cross vehicle

27/09/1992   Man became unwell whilst taking part in mountain bike race. He was a known diabetic, was given the appropriate treatment and made a speedy recovery

26/09/1992   Boy fell off mountain bike in Hamsterley forest and suffered head injuries. Taken to Bedburn in Team ambulance and to Bishop Auckland hospital in County ambulance

03/12/1991   Male in four vehicle RTA. Suffered spinal and other injuries. Team member ensured that casualty was immobilised until arrival of emergency services.

30/10/1991   Team member came across unconscious male in car in car in Lunedale. Hose pipe led from exhaust into car. Got passing motorist to alert police, ambulance and doctor. Returned to car and commenced resuscitation. Man pronounced dead by doctor.

27/10/1991	Ewe cragfast on Falcon Clints. Recovered by Team member
29/09/1991	Competitor fell from bike whilst taking part in Mountain Bike event in Hamsterley Forest. Taken to Hospital to have 9 stitches put in wound.
29/09/1991	Motor trike rider collided with telegraph post in Hamsterley Forrest. Thrown from machine and into a deep ditch. Fractured right femur. Team members assisted in giving first aid and evacuating to County Ambulance.
14/09/1991	Two youths trapped on island in River Tees near Low Force. Rescued by Team member with the assistance from farmers.
12/05/1991	Lady slipped on grass near bottom of Cauldron Snout, suspected fractured ankle. Team evacuated casualty to County ambulance
06/04/1991	Team members involved in large scale search for 3 girls missing overnight doing DofE expedition. Found safe and well next day
29/03/1991	Team members assisted 40 yr old man who collapsed in public house. Taken to hospital by ambulance.
20/03/1991	Elderly man fell down steep river bank near Scargill sustaining multiple injuries including fractured skull. Team evacuated casualty, doctor and ambulance in attendance
09/12/1990	27 dogs rescued from the back of a trailer due to drifting snow.
08/12/1990	4 People rescued from car trapped in snow drift.
07/12/1990	Search for missing person due to police locating a crashed and abandoned car in the dales.
07/12/1990	Rescue of stranded motorists from the A66 due to deep snow.
1430 03/05/1987	Search for motorcyclist after RTC, previous week - request by police to search Cockfield Fell in case of injury after crash - nothing found.
29/04/1987	Female visitor to Low Force, slipped and fell fracturing wrist. First aid given by Team member.
0800 11/04/1987	Standby to assist Cleveland SRT. Person found, mid morning in heavy rain. Team stood down at 1100hrs

21/01/1981	Mr Charles Young, a 60 year old forestry worker, was found dead on the banks of the Tees on Sunday about 100 yards from Wodencroft, Cotherstone, where he lived for the first 26 years of his life. Team members undertook a two day search for the missing man, until a body was which appeared to have been there for some months.
22/11/1979	Police were informed on Thursday night that three girl students from Sunderland Polytechnic had failed to complete a fell walk from Doctors Gate to Sharnsberry, and presumed lost somewhere on Pikeside Fell to the North of Hamsterley Forest. UTWFRA responded with 40 volunteers. It was confirmed at 3am that the girls were back in Sunderland but by then the search teams were on the fell, and it was dawn before all searchers returned to base.
19/03/1979	Expectant mother Mrs Judith Shann, of 18 Hill Terrace, Middleton was pulled nearly two miles on a sledge from Middleton to Romaldkirk on Monday afternoon because the road was blocked. Members of the Upper Teesdale fell rescue took her on their special stretcher-sledge to Romaldkirk.
21/02/1979	A blizzard was sweeping over Teesdale on Wednesday afternoon as Tom Andrews drove his small blue van through Barnard Castle and up into the dale. He was on his regular round, delivering spare parts to garages and taking orders for any equipment they needed. The van broke down and was quickly covered by heavy snow. UTWFRA team members were called to help look for the vehicle and then later for Mr Andrews who was not with the car. Team members and police searched an extensive area. Nothing found.
20/01/1979	A young expectant mother was pulled over half a mile on a sledge on Saturday after her home in Aukside, Middleton, was cut off by deep snowdrifts. The Upper Teesdale Fell Rescue team was called in and a special sledge was carried up to Mrs Galbraith. 6 Team members pulled and carried the sledge down to Middleton.
08/12/1978	HIGH FORCE HORROR. Girl, 23, plunges to death in swollen North Waterfall. The 23 year old girl fell into the river above High Force Waterfall. Members of UTWFRA pulled her body out of the river half a mile downstream.
05/07/1977	Teesdale Fell Rescue volunteers were called out on early Tuesday to take part in a search for an elderly man missing on the Cumbria side of the Pennines. He was found dead by P.C. Ken Saxby, of Mickleton, who was searching with his dog Ben. 15 volunteers from Teesdale took part.
2100 05/12/1976	Search for a male school teacher who has attempted to walk from High Force Hotel via High Cup Nick and into Dufton when he was forced to take shelter in a large snow drift. 3 Search teams involving over 200 volunteers in total along with an RAF Helicopter were involved in the search. Mr Jones awoke after a good nights sleep in the snowdrift at 10:00hrs on the Monday, started to walk back down to High Force when crossing Maize Beck he was spotted by UTWFRA Team leader Des Topping. Mr Jones was safe and well. All returned to High Force Hotel for food and lots of warm drinks.

03/07/1976   Members of UTWFRA undertook a search in the Mickle Fell area for a male Haymaker who had been overcome by the heat. Team members found the male who was suffering from severe dehydration, Salt Deficiency & cramp and transported him to Darlington memorial Hospital.

1201
12/08/1974   Team Called to assist with a Dutch tourist who had fallen in the River Tees above High Force waterfall and was holding onto a rock in the middle of the river. The male was rescued by members of UTWFRA from the river safe but soaked.

18/06/1972   Rescue Team Hauls Man From Rocks. First Action of year. A man who was taking a photograph of cauldron Snout escaped death by a few feet when he fell from the top and landed on a ledge of rock about 20 feet below.

31/03/1969   Members of Teesdale & Weardale Fell rescue Association were alerted on Monday of last week after 5 youths from the Sunderland area had failed to reach their destination at Knock, West-Morland from Langdon Beck with the prescribed time. Turned up safe & tired in Dufton at 8:45pm

12/08/1968   A party of young people were rushed by ambulance to Darlington Memorial Hospital on Monday after taking ill while walking in the High Cup Nick to Dufton area.

23/03/1968   Two young men died near High Cup Nick at the weekend, when a youth fell-walking expedition on Saturday turned into a double tragedy.

Footnote

Information regarding callouts in the early years is very sparse. We have used old records and newspaper cuttings for our information.

Should the reader have any additional information regarding callouts; or indeed any stories and anecdotes please contact us and we will try to include them in our second edition.

Acknowledgements

To all those past and present Team members who contributed to this book.

Particular thanks to Kathrine High who spent the past year collecting and compiling the information and stories contained in this book.

Our thanks to Lord Barnard for his commitment to and support of the Team during his time as Team President 1968 - 2003

Appendix

Team Leaders

1968 Team formed under chairmanship of Tom Buffey

1969 Tom Redfern

1969 to 1996 D Thompson was Team Leader,
exact start date uncertain

1996 to 2003 Alan Best

2003 on David Bartles-Smith

President

Rt Hon Harry Vane

Vice Presidents

Alan Best

Jon Stoddart

Cedric Scott

The Earl of Strathmore and Kinghome

David Thompson

Chris Scott

Ian Findlay

David Clarke

Setting up a technical rescue system -
River Tees below Low Force